ROYAL CAVALCADE

Photo: Associated Press

Princess Elizabeth and the Duke of Edinburgh at the London County Council diamond jubilee celebrations. They are seen watching the illuminations on the Thames from the steps of County Hall.

ROYAL CAVALCADE

A diary of the Royal Year

by

L. A. NICKOLLS

MACDONALD AND CO. (Publishers) LTD.
LONDON

First published 1949

*T*HIS book may serve to show, in some slight measure, how closely and at how many widely differing points the day-to-day activities of the Royal Family touch the national life.

The diary is selective, for it would not be possible, even in a far greater space than this, to take into account each and every one of countless public engagements.

If, generally, licence has been exercised in favour of the more colourful episodes, that was perhaps inevitable. Nor, of course, does the book set out to give any impression of the vast amount of work that daily goes on in private.

Made in England
PRINTED BY L. T. A. ROBINSON LTD., LONDON, S.W.9

A PRINCE IS BORN

THE LONG red-carpeted corridor that runs from the Privy Purse door of Buckingham Palace, past the rooms of the private secretaries, past the foot of the wide, winding staircase that leads upstairs to the King's study, was busy with people passing to and fro. That was unusual on a Sunday evening.

Lights shone in many of the Palace windows, adding to the expectancy of the silent London crowd that pressed up against the high iron railings of the gravelled forecourt. The Royal Standard, flying above the roof, stood out clearly in the November moonlight. The knowledgeable taxi-drivers, seeing it there, told their passengers: " That means the King's in the Palace."

Since ten o'clock, which seems early in London on a Sunday morning, there had been a steady stream of people strolling up the Mall and down Constitution Hill and round the corner from the direction of Victoria Station. All day long, people had been waiting outside the Palace and all day long they had been asking the good-natured policemen on duty there, the same questions : " Any news yet ? Think we'll get any news if we wait ? "

Some of them would stay only a few minutes, then drift away with a backward glance at the windows on the first floor. Others remained for hours. The crowd kept changing all the time. It was very noticeable that there were many more girls and women than there were men.

Now it was night-time. The deep notes of Big Ben, booming out from Westminster and across St. James's Park, struck eight. The night was pleasantly mild and free from the fog that often descends on London at this time of the year, competing murkily with the black-out of the war. All sorts and conditions of people joined the crowd. Churchpeople, coming out from Evensong, said, " I think we'll just go home past the Palace to see if there's any news." Girls with their boy friends, making for the bright lights of the West End, had the same thought. Passing motorists stopped to try to find out the latest information. There was none. All day no news had come out of the Palace.

The King and Queen had waited as anxiously as the tall, good-looking young man, the Duke of Edinburgh, who was now banging a ball about on the Palace squash court, trying to make some moments of these last dragging hours pass more quickly. There was nothing he could do. The doctors had told him they would call him immediately he was wanted. The squash racket was thrown hastily aside when, at last, he was summoned to his wife in a room on the first floor, overlooking the Mall.

The waiting was all over now. Princess Elizabeth had given birth to a son, second in the line of succession to the Throne. The Duke and the King and Queen were the first to know the great news. Queen Mary, across at Marlborough House in St. James's, was told by telephone and straightway prepared to drive to the Palace. All the members of the Royal Family were immediately informed. A message went to Whitehall to be posted on the door of the Home Office. The Lord Mayor of London, receiving the news, posted another outside the Mansion House, in the heart of the City.

The hands of the clock stood at ten minutes past ten on this night of Sunday, November 14, when my Press colleague and I were given this statement to issue to the newspapers of the world :

"*Her Royal Highness the Princess Elizabeth, Duchess of Edinburgh, was safely delivered of a Prince at 9.14 p.m. to-day.*

"*Her Royal Highness and her son are both doing well.*"

There was champagne to celebrate the birth. Still dressed in the grey flannels, cricket shirt and sweater in which he had been playing squash, the Duke received the congratulations of the members of the Household. Excitement ran the length of the long red-carpeted corridor which, normally, is not a place much given to excitement. It spread through the Palace almost as fast as rumour through a battleship.

The infant just born, whose reign may reach out into distant generations and altered days, was the first grand-child for the King and Queen. The living link stretched back through Queen Mary, soon to look upon her first great-grandchild, to the year 1867.

The people standing eight deep outside the Palace railings knew nothing of all this for the moment. Then, a little later, the discreet Privy Purse door opened, throwing a beam of light across the forecourt, and one of the Palace servants, a page with gold markings on the shoulders of his livery, came out. His name, appropriately enough, was Childs. He passed on a message from inside the Palace to the burly police superintendent who hurried across the forecourt to meet him. "It's a Prince !" he said.

"A son has been born." The police superintendent and his men told the crowd, calling out their information through the railings. "It's a Prince !" they repeated. "It's a Prince !"

All day the crowd had waited silently. But now the great cheer that went up could be heard at the other end of the Mall, in Trafalgar Square. More and more people came running to the front of the Palace, breathlessly demanding the news. For ten minutes the cheering continued without pause.

Queen Mary, upright as ever in her familiar high-backed car, drove in and the cheers broke out again. The men raised their hats to her and the women stood on tip-toe, waving. "Isn't she wonderful !" they said. Queen Mary, peering out at the mass of faces turned towards her, waved back at them. A little smile of great happiness played on her lips. Inside the Palace, the King and Queen and the Duke greeted her. She was one of the first to see the infant prince in his cradle, the same cradle that was used when Princess Elizabeth and Princess Margaret were born. There was a touch of blue about it. Blue for a boy. Everybody had been hoping the Princess and the Duke would be blessed with a son.

"We want Philip !" shouted the crowd, which was growing with every minute, now that the news had been broadcast. "We want Philip !" they kept repeating. But the Duke was with his wife.

Midnight came and still several thousand people remained. The cheering and the shouting continued. The people were so excited that they would take little notice of the police who tried to quieten the scene. Then the Duke's equerry, a friendly young man who had served with him in the Royal Navy during the war, went out to them. "Princess Elizabeth wants some rest," he said. "Prince Philip is with her and there will be nothing more to-night." Walking along inside the railings, he repeated the message at several points. The crowd understood. " Thank you, sir," they said, then melted away. Soon, only the police and the sentries were left in the moonlight.

Within the Palace, where the King walked slowly and painfully with the Queen at his side, it was quiet again. On this happy night, there was no indication for the world outside of how events were shaping and of the anxiety concerning His Majesty that was to follow the issuing of another announcement from the Palace little more than a week later.

In the early hours of Tuesday, November 23—at 1.30 a.m., when most people in England were in their beds — it was announced that the King was suffering from an obstruction to the circulation through the arteries of the legs. He had had to cancel all his public engagements for some months. The impending royal tour of Australia and New Zealand, for which all preparations had for some time been in hand, was indefinitely postponed. A doctors' bulletin made it clear that to embark upon this long journey would be hazardous and might involve serious risk to a limb. The defective blood supply to the right foot was causing anxiety, said the doctors. Complete rest had been advised. Though the King's general health, including the condition of his heart, gave no reason for concern, there was no doubt that the strain of the past twelve years of kingship had " appreciably affected his resistance to physical fatigue." The news came as a shock at home and overseas. Messages of sympathy and hope for a speedy recovery poured into Buckingham Palace from all over the world.

The following Sunday morning, a few passers-by in quiet Chester Square, a mile or so from the Palace, saw one of the royal cars driving through the thick fog with side-lights on. At St. Michael's Church, where a clergyman waited at the side door, the Queen and Princess Margaret stepped from the car and went inside to join the con-gregation at their morning service. Before the customary prayers for the sick, the National Anthem was sung. " Sing it as a prayer," the clergyman told his congregation.

The King remained at the Palace for two months. Though forced to spend most of his time in bed at first, he continued even then to deal with his State papers and correspondence in the usual way. Few people realise for what long hours a King, in these days, is tied to his desk. Every day, for much of the time, the Queen sat at his bedside. She took most of her meals in the King's room.

" God bless the Queen ! " cried the crowd when, with her younger daughter, Princess Margaret, and her son-in-law, the Duke of Edinburgh, to support her, she left the Palace to carry out her first public engagement in London after the announcement of the King's illness.

As the December days wore on, the news of the King became more reassuring. The jury of doctors was able to report that he was improving, an announcement received with thankfulness everywhere.

Meanwhile, the infant Prince had steadily been putting on weight and there was considerable oral evidence available that he was the possessor of a good and healthy pair of lungs. He was christened Charles Philip Arthur George in the Music Room of the Palace on December 15, the day following the fifty-third birthday of the King who was present as one of the sponsors. For this ceremony the baby was dressed in the historic christening robe of Honiton lace worn by all Queen Victoria's children. Queen Victoria gave it to Queen Mary in 1894. The King wore it at his baptism and so did all his brothers and his sister, the Princess Royal. It was brought out once more for Princess Elizabeth and again for Princess Margaret. The children of the Duke and Duchess of Gloucester and of the Duchess of Kent and the late Duke of Kent all wore it. The

The first photograph of Prince Charles, seen in his mother's arms after the christening. He had eight sponsors, six of whom are shown here.

Queen Mary and the Dowager Marchioness of Milford Haven are seated with Princess Elizabeth. Standing with the King are : Lady Brabourne, the Duke of Edinburgh (who stood proxy for Prince George of Greece), the Hon. David Bowes-Lyon (brother of the Queen), the Earl of Athlone (who stood proxy for King Haakon of Norway) and Princess Margaret.

latest wearer of the robe behaved very well at his christening ; then, apparently having had sufficient excitement for one day, he went to sleep while the photographs were being taken.

1948 eked out its last days. For the first time since he came to the Throne, the King spent Christmas in London. There was a quiet family gathering at the Palace where, this time, the Music Room served as a chapel for morning service. The King's broadcast in the afternoon of Christmas Day was generally regarded as the best he has ever made.

Early in the New Year, Londoners had their first glimpse of Prince Charles, now seven weeks old. Princess Elizabeth, the Duke of Edinburgh and Princess Margaret were setting out for a holiday at Sandringham. Princess Elizabeth took Prince Charles with her, nursing him on the back seat of the car, while the Duke drove with Princess Margaret at his side in the front. The baby's nurse sat with Princess Elizabeth. So they set off for Norfolk, in holiday mood.

No one who saw them driving out so happily will ever forget to boast : " I saw the young Prince Charles in his mother's arms the very first day she ever took him out. A little mite he was, all wrapped up in a white woollen shawl and the Princess nursing him as though he was the most precious thing on earth—which, for her, he undoubtedly was."

And then, a few days later, after eight weeks of confinement within the Palace, the King joined the Princesses and the Duke at Sandringham, travelling with the Queen by train from London. His car was driven on to the platform at King's Cross station, so that he had only to step out of it into the train. He looked pale and wan. But, despite everything, he had a kindly smile for the officials who were there to see him off.

Good news came from Sandringham of the progress of the King's convalescence as January gave way to February. Towards the end of that month His Majesty returned to London.

Privileged to follow the royal year, I kept a diary of some of its events, from which is selected what follows in this volume.

Photo: Daily Graphic

Off to Sandringham. Prince Charles leaves the Palace for the first time.

RETURN OF THE KING

THURSDAY, FEBRUARY 24, 1949. The King came back to London this afternoon; and the Royal Standard flies again from the flagstaff of Buckingham Palace.

There was something very affecting about this quiet return after nearly seven weeks of rest at Sandringham. It was an afternoon with a touch of Spring about it. One felt that, even in the London air. The crowds gathered in the sharp February sunshine outside King's Cross railway station and outside the Palace. The day lent brightness to the murky station and added its own kindliness to the welcome back. It is always pleasant, whether you be King or commoner, to arrive in sunshine.

It was a quiet occasion, for this was a " private " return. The long Number One platform was practically empty. But, at the end of it—back behind the white barrier at the platform entrance and pressed against the tobacco kiosk and the telephone boxes—a crowd had gathered. There were hundreds more out in the street, glad to see the King back.

On Number One platform, the railway executives and the high police officials waited and chatted, glancing now and then at the platform clock. The stationmaster had put on his glossiest silk hat. Two porters gave the platform its final sweeping.

In came the green-painted " Royal Sovereign," pulling the " Sandringham Special " with its brown, white-topped carriages. It was three minutes late, an unusual enough occurrence to cause comment among those on the platform.

The red carpet was down but that was the only touch of ceremonial about the friendly and informal scene that followed. First out of the train, hurrying with six red-leather despatch boxes to the waiting car, was a page in the blue battle-dress style of uniform introduced at the Palace during the war. These boxes would contain papers on which the King had been working at Sandringham. Following the page, another royal servant slipped unobtrusively from the train, carrying rugs and umbrellas.

The King stepped out a moment later. He was cheerful and smiling and looked slightly fuller in the face than when he went away. It was grand to see His Majesty in such good heart. There seemed only the slightest suggestion of a limp in his walk. The Queen, dressed in one of her favourite colours, dove grey, came out of the train behind the King. The railway officials bowed and the police came to the salute. Then, while the King and Queen stood chatting on the platform, that engaging little dog, " Crackers," was led from the train to the car. " Crackers," a corgi, and pet of the whole Royal Family, travels in style.

Outside the station, the crowds cheered as the King and Queen drove away and, momentarily, the flashlights of the photographers lit up the dark exit. Past the boarding houses and the private hotels of the Bloomsbury area, into Trafalgar Square with its busy fountains, through Admiralty Arch and up the familiar Mall to the

Palace, they drove, passing below the garden windows of Queen Mary's residence, Marlborough House, and past Clarence House, now being prepared for its new tenants, Princess Elizabeth and the Duke of Edinburgh.

Up on the roof of the Palace, the King's flagman spotted the royal car as it came through the arch. He waited until it passed through the gateway into the forecourt. At that precise moment the Royal Standard fluttered out in the light afternoon breeze and, flying there above the Palace, informed all and sundry that His Majesty was in residence.

TUESDAY, MARCH 1, 1949. The investiture which the King held at Buckingham Palace to-day was the first ceremony in which he has taken part since last November when his illness became acute. Throughout all these long, anxious weeks, he has been carrying on with his desk work. The Prime Minister, Mr. Attlee, and others have been received in audience and there have been two Privy Councils, one at the Palace and the other at Sandringham House.

Of the 296 people summoned to the investiture, all but about fifty had figured in the New Year's Honours List, the appearance of which in January had been as eagerly awaited as ever, alike by the ambitious and the deserving.

Outside, the sightseers who clustered round the gateway to watch the arrivals came muffled and wrapped against the bitter east wind which hinted at snow. Inside, in the State drawing room and galleries, cheerful fires burned in the white marble fireplaces. For the first time since the war, the State ballroom, with its memories of pre-war Courts and nervous, curtseying debutantes, was being used for an investiture. This room was built for Queen Victoria between 1853 and 1855. It is the largest of all the State apartments ; 123 feet long, 60 feet wide and 45 feet to the white and

gold ceiling. It set an impressive stage for to-day's ceremony. On the royal dais stand the two thrones under a canopy of crimson velvet, embroidered in gold with the Imperial Crown, the Royal Cipher and the Royal Arms. Six large rose-tinted chandeliers light the room. Tapestries on the walls depict scenes from the story of Jason and the Golden Fleece.

Up in the musicians' gallery, a string band of the Scots Guards, the bandsmen in their scarlet tunics, played its light music ; a minuet, a waltz, selections from the *Lilac Domino*. There is never anything heavy or formal about the musical programmes for investitures. The music provides a quiet, tuneful background for the general scene.

Six hundred guests came to watch their relatives decorated by the King, entering by way of the Grand Entrance from which Princess Elizabeth set out for the Abbey on her wedding day fifteen months ago. They climbed the wide, red-carpeted stairway to the East Gallery, then passed through to the ballroom. The spectators soon filled the tiers of long rose-coloured damask seats around the walls. The remainder had chairs on the ballroom floor.

On these occasions, everybody receiving an award or decoration is allowed to bring two guests and no more. One can well believe that this firm rule must have caused a good deal of discussion in many a family circle. Who is to go ? And who is to stand down ? To-day the guests were mainly women, as is usually the case. There was, though, a fair sprinkling of children ; all of them very thrilled and exceedingly spick and span. They were awed into such silence that they would scarcely whisper to their mothers.

The behind-the-scene arrangements are interesting. While the onlookers assemble in the ballroom, the " recipients," as they are officially styled, gather in the picture gallery, with its Van Dyck and Rubens paintings. Officials from the Lord Chamberlain's Office and from the Central

Chancery of the Orders of Knighthood marshal them into separate, roped-off enclosures and then form them up in the order in which they are to be called before the King. One man out of place might upset everything. The officials, however, are old hands at all this. Long experience and an elaborate system of checking and counter-checking obviates mistakes, though there was one occasion when things went a little wrong. That was when the name of a well-known R.A.F. Air-Marshal having been called out, a middle-aged woman was found standing next in line, all ready to step before the King.

Eleven o'clock is the invariable hour for the start of an investiture. All those being decorated have to be there well beforehand. Some of them get very nervous. Men being decorated for bravery will confess, " I didn't sleep half the night, dreaming I might make some awful boob." They all seem to forget their nervousness when their turns come. And no one has ever been known to make any " awful boob."

One has seen many investitures but this ceremony to-day was especially impressive since it so clearly demonstrated the King's determination to carry on despite his illness. He conducted it sitting in a small chair so as to relieve the strain on his legs.

Punctually, on the stroke of eleven, he entered the ballroom, dressed in the uniform of Admiral of the Fleet. He walked slowly to the centre of the royal dais, then turned to face the room. Watching from the musicians' gallery, the bandmaster could time this as the exact moment for the beginning of the National Anthem.

" Will you be seated, ladies and gentle-men," said the King when this was ended ; and he himself took his seat on the small chair, placed towards the front of the dais. Normally, he would remain standing. Members of the Royal Household in attendance were grouped around him. Stalwarts of the King's Bodyguard of the Yeomen of

the Guard, in their picturesque uniforms, stood guard on the dais.

With the Guards' musicians continuing their light music, the investiture began. An Admiral led the way, standing before the King to receive the insignia of a Knight Grand Cross of the Most Honourable Order of the Bath. An Army General followed him. In normal circumstances, the King would place the ribands and badges of the Orders about their necks but to-day, to avoid standing, he handed them all the insignia in cases.

For an hour and a quarter the ceremony continued with all its categories of honour within the different Orders—The Most Honourable Order of the Bath, the Most Distinguished Order of Saint Michael and Saint George, the Royal Victorian Order, the Most Excellent Order of the British Empire. The Victorian Order, together with the six-hundred-years-old Most Noble Order of the Garter, are two Orders in which there are no political appointments ; they are in the absolute gift of the Sovereign. Another is the Order of Merit.

The greatest general interest centred in the new knights who came " to receive the Honour of Knighthood." There were fifty-eight of them altogether. Of this number, thirty-one were Knights Bachelor. They come within none of the Orders and, incidentally, receive no insignia, though they may purchase an approved badge from the Imperial Society of Knights Bachelor.

The actual ceremony of knighting takes no more than half a minute. Each new knight, upon being announced, steps forward in front of the King. He bows, then kneels before his Sovereign on a small red plush stool. The King takes his ceremonial.sword from his equerry and touches the kneeling figure on each shoulder, whereupon the new knight arises with the title " Sir." It may well have taken him a lifetime to earn the honour.

The Admirals and the Generals and the Air Marshals gave way to those of lesser rank. There came nurses, police constables and civilians. The King had a handshake and a word of congratulation for each of them.

There was a special word for a brave and youthful sailor who came near the end. This lad—Boy (First Class) Alfred Lowe, formerly of H.M.S. Illustrious—swam to the rescue of a midshipman when one of the ship's liberty boats capsized and sank in a storm. That dark, desperate night must have seemed like some half-forgotten nightmare to Boy Lowe as he stood before the King amid all this magnificence to receive the Albert Medal for his bravery.

Photo: Planet News

After the investiture. Boy Lowe outside Buckingham Palace.

FRIDAY, MARCH 4, 1949. While the King was holding the investiture at Buckingham Palace, Princess Elizabeth and her husband began a three-days' visit to Edinburgh. They returned to London this morning, travelling in the wake of reports that indicated they had stirred this great and dignified Scottish city to its heart. For the first time, the Princess's personal standard flew above the Palace of Holyroodhouse, where they went into residence on Tuesday morning ; and for the first time the city saw the Princess and the Duke who bears its name as husband and wife.

There were great ceremonies. The Duke received the Freedom of the City, the Princess the honorary degree of Doctor of Laws from the University. Both were admitted honorary members of a Company formed many years ago to establish order and fair dealing in the cloth trade, the Edinburgh Merchant Company, whose charter was granted in the year 1681.

Away from all ceremony, we find them visiting some cottages for old people ; and there, chatting with seventy-eight-years-old Jenny Black and her sister, Agnes, the Duke suggests, after a little while : " I think you had better go in out of the cold now." Those two old ladies will talk about this day for the rest of their lives.

Looking out upon the world to-day, the young Princess declared at the University : " It is not surprising that my generation grows rather more serious in purpose than some of its predecessors. Indeed we must be, for ours is a tremendous responsibility. We have been born in times when great institutions have crumbled, age-old traditions have been called in question, and science has produced horrors to keep pace with its marvels."

And, looking into the future, one of the University professors told the Princess : " It is our prayer that in the fullness of time, under your guidance, there may dawn

Photo: The Scotsman

During the Edinburgh visit. A happy picture of Princess Elizabeth greeting an old lady at the Lockerby Cottages.

Photo: Scottish Daily Record

An incident during the visit to Edinburgh in March.

17   B

Photo : The Scotsman

Inspecting the guard of the King's Own Scottish Borderers at the Palace of Holyrood-house, Edinburgh.

Photo : The Bulletin

The visit to Edinburgh. The Duke during an inspection of a parade of Youth organisations.

18

for Britain a second Elizabethan Age which, in its grandeur, will outshine its predecessor."

TUESDAY, MARCH 8, 1949. The great State occasions of any year are always deeply impressive. But it is more often in the vast variety of the smaller events, unrehearsed and unspectacular, that one comes across those warm-hearted little scenes and stories that mirror the kindliness of our Royal Family.

To-day, for instance, the Queen drove up to St. John's Wood to open a new block of flats in Cochrane Street, near that centre of the cricketing world, Lord's. The flags were up in the street, the crowds gathered and the Queen went from flat to flat, making her customary very thorough inspection.

"I wonder if Her Majesty would like a cup of tea?" asked one of the housewives, half-way through the afternoon's visit. The Queen said she would. She was shown into the small dining-room while the housewife hurried off to her kitchen. The kettle was already on the boil and soon the good woman was back with the Queen's tea. She was so flustered that it was not until then that she realised she had made it in her old brown teapot instead of her best one.

Later, when she had watched the Queen enter her big, shining car to drive back to the Palace, the woman went back to her dining-room. She found a pencil and marked a cross on the bottom of the armchair in which the Queen had been sitting. "So that I don't get it mixed up with the other one of the pair," she said. Later she would have a plaque made, she planned, and she'd put it on the chair. It was now her most-prized piece of furniture. She smiled to herself at the thought.

Photo: Associated Press

March 9 : The Queen and Princess Elizabeth at an exhibition of Dutch and Flemish pictures in London.

Then she remembered the old brown teapot. What a silly thing that had been to do ! " *But I think the Queen would understand how it could happen, don't you ?* " she asked me when I called.

WEDNESDAY, MARCH 10, 1949. Princess Margaret, who will be nineteen in August, has just started a series of private and informal visits which have been taking her here and there about London. She wants to see things for herself. These visits, which began with a tour of inspection of that somewhat mysterious and forbidding place, the

Battersea power station, on the south side of the Thames, form part of the training of a Royal Princess in the twentieth century.

Within the last few days Princess Margaret has been to hear her first debate in the House of Commons (she has sent to her daily when the House is in session a copy of Hansard which gives a verbatim report of the proceedings), has attended a session of a Juvenile Court in East London and has been shown some—but not all—of the secrets of Scotland Yard.

On another occasion, accompanying the

Photo: Planet News

The Queen and Princess Margaret during the inspection of the cargo ship *Port Brisbane*.

Queen, the Princess drove to the London docks to inspect a new Newcastle-built cargo boat, the *Port Brisbane*, trading between the United Kingdom and Australia and New Zealand. The first vessel to bear this name was sunk in the Indian Ocean by a German raider in 1940. This new ship, 12,500 tons, is the first stream-lined cargo boat to trade to Australasia, claim her owners, who also point out that one of her shiploads would provide the meat ration for the entire population of the United Kingdom for two days.

The Queen led the way and the Princess followed during an inspection lasting an hour and a half which took them down into one of the holds, into the galley, where the cooks were preparing a meal, and through the crew's quarters. Old sailors, one imagines, would stare amazed at this crew accommodation in a cargo boat. Petty officers are in single berth cabins and not more than two seamen are berthed in any one cabin. The crew has a recreation room and a separate reading and writing room.

The ship had come from Newcastle in a gale which had tested her well. Water in the King George V dock, rising three and a half feet above normal, set officials of the Port Line worrying about the possibility of having to ask the Queen and the Princess to go up a gangway tilted at a somewhat alarming angle. Fortunately, the flood water went down.

Princess Margaret wore for this visit a most attractive new ensemble. Over a matching red frock, she had on a long, full cherry-red coat with a black astrakhan collar falling over the shoulders like a small cape. Her red cloche hat carried a black eagle's feather. Black handbag and shoes completed a delightful picture. Everybody commented how charming she looked.

And now, to-day, Princess Elizabeth has taken her younger sister to the Central Criminal Court. When they drove up Ludgate Hill to the grim Old Bailey, as it is

Photo: Evening Standard

"*Princess Margaret wore for this visit a most attractive new ensemble . . .*"

more widely known, the two Princesses made history. They were the first members of the Royal Family to visit the court since their great-grandfather, King Edward VII, opened it forty-two years ago.

In Number One Court, scene of so many famous cases, they listened to the trial of two men accused of attempting to murder two police officers by running them down in a van which, it was alleged by the prosecution, had been stolen.

Everybody in Court stood when the Princesses entered, to take their seats behind the barristers' benches. They, in their turn, rose with everybody else when the Lord Chief Justice of England, Lord Goddard, robed in scarlet and ermine, came on to the Bench. In this place His Majesty's judge took precedence over the King's daughters.

For the first time in their lives, the Princesses heard a jury sworn in, the jurors swearing on oath that they would " well and truly try, and true deliverance make, between our Sovereign Lord, the King, and the prisoner at the Bar. . . . And a true verdict give, according to the evidence."

They remained until the mid-day adjournment, listening to prosecuting counsel's outline of the case and to the evidence and cross-examination of witnesses called for the Crown. Watching the slow, relentless working of the law, they seemed deeply impressed.

SATURDAY, MARCH 12, 1949. The King to-day underwent an operation, known as lumbar sympathectomy, to free the flow of blood to his right foot. Not a dangerous operation, the doctors had said ; but there is always some anxiety attaching to any operation. It was a happy duty, therefore, to send out the first bulletin indicating that all was well. " His Majesty's condition," it said, " is entirely satisfactory." The news, flashed round the world in a matter of minutes, was received with relief by millions of people. This evening there was a second and equally reassuring bulletin. The King had had a restful day following the operation, stated the doctors. Temperature, pulse and respiration had not varied from normal.

Everybody has admired the way in which the King has faced this illness, carrying on with his desk work all the time, receiving official visitors in audience and holding the investiture last week. Let us hope that now we shall see him steadily on the mend.

SUNDAY, MARCH 13, 1949. Another bulletin this morning. Good news again, one was happy to be able to record. The doctors are obviously very satisfied with the progress that the King is making, for they did not return this evening.

A cold, grey day but many people braved this cheerless March weather to wait outside the Palace, at the railings, for news of the King. What is it that brings them there ? Talk to them and you will find that it is not mere curiosity. Respect, affection, sympathy leads them and they wait in the cold and the rain, a quiet and patient crowd of well-wishers.

They cheered the Queen when, in the late afternoon, she drove down the Mall to Marlborough House to have tea with Queen Mary.

FRIDAY, MARCH 25, 1949. To get to Canning Town, you drive through the East End of London ; along the interminable length of the Commercial Road, then by way of that romantic-sounding thoroughfare, the East India Dock Road. So, at last, you will come to Canning Town. Twist and turn among the bomb-blitzed streets and, where postmen deliver letters marked " London E. 16," you will find the Dockland Settlement which the Duke of Edinburgh visited to-night. That it is not easy to find is clear from the fact that the car from Buckingham Palace lost its way in the side streets.

Meet the grey-haired local reporter and he will be able to recall for you the days when, from two slum houses and a tin

His Majesty the King.

Photo: Associated Press

March 16.   The Duchess of Kent visits a junior club of the Save the Children Fund in
Eversholt Street, London.

church, the Malvern Mission set about its work of doing good among the people of these poor, dark streets. That was before the 1914 war. From those small beginnings, the organization spread its influence wider and wider as the years went on. To-day the Settlement, with all its branches, touches the lives of many thousands. They will tell you at Canning Town that no one is too young or too old for one or other of their clubs. Whether you be a child in arms or a grandfather, they have something for you.

It was to see some of the younger lads boxing that the Duke, himself a keen sportsman, went to Canning Town to-night, accompanied by his equerry, the friendly Lieutenant Michael Parker, of the Royal Navy. The local boys were taking on lads from three other boxing clubs. Twenty short, three-round fights followed one

Photo: Daily Graphic

March 19 : Princess Elizabeth and the Duke of Edinburgh watch 2,000 students in costume, parade in a pageant " Students through the ages ", in Hyde Park, London.

another in quick succession in the little theatre, rigged up for the occasion. Mothers, fathers, brothers, sisters looked on. There were frequent shouts of encouragement for " Good old Bert " or " Good old Harry." Boxing is taken very seriously in this part of the world and these youngsters ducked and weaved and feinted with a hundred and one small imitations of the professionals. Their boxing trunks held all the colours of the rainbow. The trainers in their white flannels and singlets watched from their respective corners as keenly as though a world championship was at stake. The little boys obviously took that view, too. The trainers were complete with all the paraphernalia of gum-shields, sponges, towels. They whipped their galvanised iron pails and enamel basins into the corners the

moment the bell sounded at the end of a round ; gave their juvenile principals a quick swig from their bottles of water ; whispered urgent words of advice, illustrated by wicked-looking short-arm jabs. And, while the seconds fanned furiously with their towels, the boy boxers stole occasional quick glances at the corner opposite to see how the other fellow was getting on.

Everyone felt terribly sorry for the little lad whose singlet—put on back to front and far too big for him anyway—kept slipping off his shoulder every time he went into action. He was as much worried by the singlet as he was by his opponent. The combination defeated him. Then there was the bewildered boy who had to be declared a winner without a fight. The opposing second took a quick glance at him, decided

25

apparently that he was over age or too big for his boy, whom he promptly proceeded to withdraw from the ring.

"G'arn," said the other boy's uncle to his friend at the ringside. "His age is all right. Didn't I go to his birthday last week?" But by this time, the unwilling one was already well out of the hall. In the end, they all went into the ring again, winners and losers, to get their prizes from the Duke.

It was getting on for midnight when the Duke drove back to Buckingham Palace, passing the lighted East End jellied eel stalls on his way. Even at this hour they were doing a good trade. The customers were so intent on their delicacies that the royal car passed quite unnoticed. In his pocket, the Duke's equerry carried two little presents—a bib and a bangle for young Prince Charles from the children of dockland.

Photo: Photographic News

" Where postmen deliver letters marked ' London, E. 16 ', you will find the Dockland Settlement."
The Duke of Edinburgh with some of the boy boxers at Canning Town.

March 28 : A Bristol street scene. The Princess, the Lord Mayor and the Guard of Honour.

PRINCESS MARGARET PAYS A VISIT TO BRISTOL

At the Youth Exhibition. Boat-building by Bristol Boy Scouts and Sea Scouts. Work stops when the Princess visits their stand.

At Downend Children's Homes.

Photos:
  Evening World

Photo: P. A. Harding

March 29 : Princess Margaret goes hunting before returning to London after her Bristol tour. Riding with her is the Duchess of Beaufort.

Photo: Evening World

March 27 : Leaving Badminton Church, after attending morning service there on the Sunday.

WEDNESDAY, MARCH 30, 1949. There ended in Manchester this evening, at 6.10 p.m., when the Royal train pulled out from London Road station, two very remarkable days. I cannot recall, outside London since the end of the war, crowd scenes such as we have witnessed during this visit to Lancashire. First Liverpool, then Preston, and today, the great city of Manchester have given the Princess and the Duke tremendous welcomes. At times, the crowds took matters into their own hands. Carefully planned schedules were swept aside. At one stage, the royal visitors, held up by this great reception, were nearly two hours late. They were cheered from morning till night by countless thousands who turned out in the sunshine to wish them well.

It was the first time that the Princess and her husband had visited this part of the country together. And, together, they won most people's hearts. The visit seemed to bring colour and romance wherever it touched. There was a happiness in the air that one seldom sees in the world nowadays. Even in the poorest of the dark streets, everybody seemed to be smiling, laughing. At times it was like the wedding day all over again. There was magic in it, I do declare.

A combination of feelings led to these remarkable demonstrations. First and foremost, people wanted to see the Princess and the Duke. And, having taken a look at the young couple, they liked them ; and showed in no uncertain way that they liked them. There was a deeper note in it, too. Here was sympathy for the King in his illness, expressed to him indirectly through this great welcome to his daughter and his

Photo: Liverpool Daily Post

" *I declare this lock open and wish God speed to the ships that pass through it and to those who sail in them.*" Opening the new lock at Liverpool.

son-in-law. Princess Elizabeth herself said that she had seldom seen crowds like this.

These tumultuous street scenes provided the background for the more formal side of the programme. There was the opening of a new £1,000,000 lock in the Liverpool docks on the first day. The Princess, standing with the Duke on the bridge of the Mersey Docks and Harbour Board's tender, the 569 tons Galatea, made what is thought to be the first royal public speech from a moving vessel when she said : "*I declare this lock open and wish God speed to the ships that pass through it and to those who sail in them.*" The Duke took on the after-luncheon speech at the Town Hall, replying "on behalf of my wife and myself" to the welcome of the Lord Mayor. Alderman W. T. Lancashire, who holds this high office, is obviously most fittingly named.

The Duke made one of his pleasantly informal speeches. He recalled how, as a schoolboy, he had listened to a lantern-slide lecture about Liverpool Cathedral and had made up his mind that one day he must visit it. "But I never imagined that it

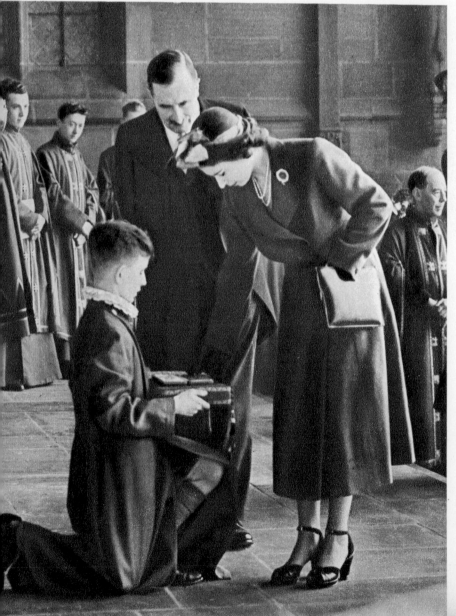

A kneeling choirboy offers Princess Elizabeth the key of the great door of Liverpool Cathedral.

Photo: Graphic Photo Union

"*The great cathedral that is slowly rising above the Liverpool rooftops.*" Princess Elizabeth and the Duke coming down the cathedral steps.

Photo: Kemsley Newspapers

would be in these circumstances," he said ; and he smiled across at the Princess.

There is much else that stands out in the memory of this day in Liverpool. Who is there who was present who will ever forget the heavenly singing of that choir in the great cathedral that is slowly rising above the Liverpool rooftops ? There are old men working in the stone-masons' yard adjoining the cathedral who will tell you how they first went there over forty years ago, when nothing stood above the ground. Now the carved stone pinnacles tower hundreds of feet above the patient masons, still tapping and chiselling in the yard below. There will be many more years of building yet ; but how many no-one seemed to be able to say. The young choirboys who sang so beautifully to-day will pass into manhood as they watch the cathedral grow.

Inside this great church, the Princess and the Duke stencilled their initials—E and P —on one of the stones of the pillar of the lower nave. There the letters will remain, cut out of the enduring stone and entwined in a true lovers' knot, as long as the pillar

stands. Perhaps in centuries to come, people visiting this place will weave a fairy-tale around them for their children, if by then there is any enchantment left in the world.

The small congregation was asked to offer in silence this ancient prayer as the Princess and the Duke were about to leave :

Farewell.
You have God's blessing
And mine.
I pray Almighty God that
True peace
Perfect guidance
Spiritual Strength
And an abundance of Grace
May evermore be with you
And all God's lovers
In the countries of your love.
Amen.

The young schoolboy, Philip, planning in his youth to visit the cathedral, could never have dreamed of all this, nor of the scenes that followed. Thousands upon thousands of people, finishing work, swelled the crowds filling the streets as the Princess and the Duke drove out of Liverpool, making for Preston, thirty miles away. For seven consecutive miles they travelled at no more than a walking pace. At times their car was brought to a standstill, its passage blocked by great masses of cheering men, women and children. Preston was reached, nearly two hours late, in the gathering dusk instead of at tea-time. Here again, there were scenes of wild enthusiasm in which more than one policeman lost his helmet. The Princess, one imagines, must have been very glad of that cup of tea at the Harris Art Gallery.

At dinner at the County Hall that night, red roses of Lancaster decorated the table and, as at lunchtime, the loyal toast was given in this form : " The King, Duke of Lancaster." Two hundred and thirty-two years ago, within a mile of so of the place where the dinner was held, the reigning

monarch of England spent a few brief but pleasant hours, recalled the Lord Lieutenant of the County Palatine of Lancaster, Earl Peel. On that occasion the menu for the banquet contained a choice of fifty-two dishes. " One of them at least achieved some degree of notoriety," declared the Lord Lieutenant. His reference was to the story that James the First, having been invited to dinner by one of his nobles, drew his sword and knighted the joint of beef set before him. Thus, it is said, it became known as " Sir-loin." Other stories attribute the knighting to other monarchs, one of these being Henry the Eighth.

So on to Manchester for the second day of this Lancashire visit. The sun shone ; and that, in Manchester, is rare enough to be recorded. There were spring flowers— primroses and daffodils—in the Garden of Remembrance in St. Peter's Square, dedicated in the presence of the Princess and the Duke to all Manchester men and women and children who died in the recent war. The memorial is an oasis set in the heart of the city. The bright, gay colours of the garden stood out clear and fresh against the grimed stone of the Manchester buildings. In the morning sunshine, there were prayers and hymns and the reading of a Lesson. One of the prayers, which was for the soul of this great city of Manchester, might well apply to many another community. . . . " Grant us a vision of our City, fair as she might be ; a city of justice, where none shall prey on others ; a city of plenty, where vice and poverty shall cease to fester ; a city of brotherhood, where all success shall be founded on service, and honour shall be given to nobleness alone ; a city of peace, where order shall not rest on force, but on the love of all for the city, the great mother of the common life and weal." Amen, murmured the men and women of Manchester who filled the square.

This quiet and solemn note changed. Each crowded street roared its welcome as the Princess and the Duke drove on. They came eventually to the poor and seamy side of the city ; a young and fresh and lovely girl, with her mother's smile and laughing, dancing eyes, riding through these drab grey streets at the side of the handsome young naval lieutenant with whom she fell in love. It made you feel happier just to look at them and the crowds cheered them all the more for choosing to come this way and brighten the day for everybody.

In this district is Every Street. No doubt the Princess and the Duke were told the city's stock joke : " We have been in *every* street in Manchester." One likes to think that they may have tried it out on the King and Queen when they got back to the Palace.

With Manchester's woman Lord Mayor at a new block of flats.
Photo: Daily Express

" *The crowds cheered them all the more for choosing to come this way and brighten the day for everybody.*"
Photo: Kemsley Newspapers

DIARY FOR APRIL

WEDNESDAY, APRIL 6, 1949. The King, everyone is thankful to hear, continues to make good progress after his recent operation. The doctors, however, have advised that a prolonged period of convalescence will be necessary, so that His Majesty will be carrying out no public engagements yet. To-day, he and the Queen left London for Royal Lodge, that quiet retreat in Windsor Great Park, where a comfortable homeliness in the way of life supplants any formality or ceremony.

They drove out of Buckingham Palace during the afternoon, while at Westminster, a mile or so away across St. James's Park, the Chancellor of the Exchequer, Sir Stafford Cripps, was presenting his austerity Budget to a crowded House of Commons. The King already knew Sir Stafford's secrets. They were disclosed to him yesterday, twenty-four hours in advance of the speech, when he received the Chancellor in private audience at the Palace. This is customary. What a multitude of secrets must have been unfolded in that audience chamber on the first floor, overlooking the garden and Constitution Hill ! But those walls have no ears.

FRIDAY, APRIL 8, 1949. " Dinners are made for eating, not talking," you will find it stated in " Fashnable Fax and Polite Annygoats," which forms part of Thackeray's " Yellowplush Correspondence."

Whether the Duke of Edinburgh, who seems nowadays to be the principal diner-out in the Royal Family, would agree with that statement, I do not pretend to know. Certain it is that he does his full share of after-dinner speech-making and seems to take it very comfortably in his stride. He speaks in the direct, straightforward manner of the sailor, usually using no more than a few notes jotted down on a slip of paper. He likes to make what he says catch the spirit and feeling of the occasion rather than prepare a set formal speech beforehand. His voice is deep and attractive, his style friendly, easy and informal.

All sorts of organizations ask his support and attendance. To-night, for instance, there was an appeal dinner to raise funds for the British Schools Exploring Society which seeks through its overseas expeditions to stimulate the spirit of adventure among British lads. This was just the sort of enterprise to appeal to the Duke. He gave it his full backing and recalled during his speech one or two schoolboy adventures of his own. One gets the impression that as a boy he was pretty well game for anything. The evening was memorable for an inspiring speech by the adventurous Lord Mountevans —better known as " Evans of the Broke "— who was a member of Scott's ill-fated Antarctic expedition.

" As it happens," said Lord Mountevans, " I was the last man who is alive to-day to speak to Captain Scott, far away in the uttermost South. And for more than thirty-seven years I have had as my greatest

Photo: Keystone

The Duke of Edinburgh shakes hands with John Mills, the actor, who played the leading part in the film, " Scott of the Antarctic ". An incident at the appeal dinner of the British Schools Exploring Society.

inspiration in peace and war that last message of his, when, after the longest sledge journey in history, he wrote with the pencil dropping from his frozen fingers : ' How much better has all this been than lounging in too great comfort at home.' "

Now, the Master Tailors' Benevolent Association dinner, another of these functions that the Duke has attended, was in lighter vein. Largely, the subject of the speeches was clothes ; men's clothes. " It is sometimes said that it is the clothes that make the man," declared the President of the Association. " We have here to-night the men who make the clothes that make the man." He said he thought the Duke was " a perfect example of how a Britisher should be dressed on all occasions."

The Duke looked round the tables at the master tailors. They included, of course, his own tailor. " As perhaps the only customer here, I want to say that though you may make the clothes, we have to wear 'em," said he. " I think your greatest contribution as tailors is to make comfortable clothes. And if you gentlemen make them," he added with a nice diplomatic touch, " we know that they'll be smart, too." The Duke's presence resulted in a record attendance at the dinner and this in turn was reflected in the sum raised for the benevolent fund.

The King, as Duke of York, had his full round of public dinners of this kind. Now he does not dine out publicly. Two of the Royal Dukes—the Duke of Gloucester and the Duke of Edinburgh—bear the brunt of the after-dinner speech making.

35

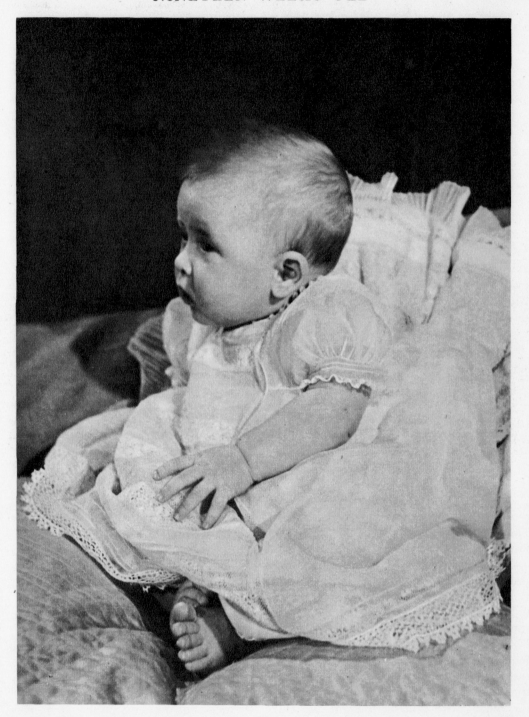

Photo: Baron

Prince Charles of Edinburgh was nineteen weeks old when this photograph was taken.
He weighed 16 lbs. 2 ozs.

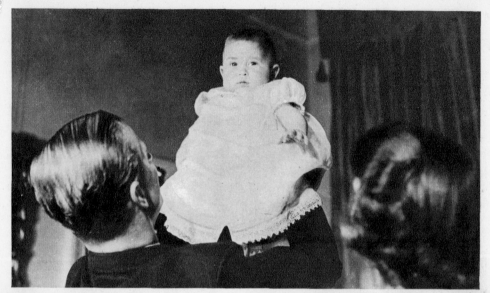

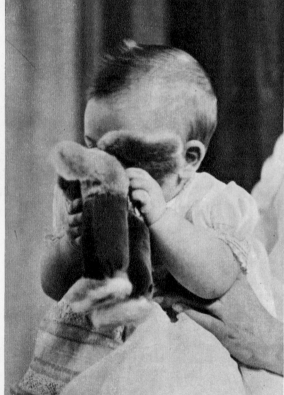

Photos: Baron

Says the diarist : " *The infant Prince Charles of Edinburgh—now affectionately, if somewhat informally, known as ' Good Old Charlie ' from one end of the country to the other —continues to prosper in health and to put on weight in the most satisfactory manner.   He is the apple of his mother's eye and the country's darling.   Everywhere nowadays, they toast Prince Charles.*"

37

SUNDAY, APRIL 10, 1949. It is twenty-one weeks since that exciting Sunday night of November the fourteenth when Princess Elizabeth's baby was born. The infant Prince Charles of Edinburgh—now affectionately, if somewhat informally, known as " Good Old Charlie " from one end of the country to the other—continues to prosper in health and to put on weight in the most satisfactory manner. He is the apple of his mother's eye and the country's darling. Everywhere nowadays they toast Prince Charles.

back from all these mothers a flow of letters, written on all sorts and shapes and sizes and scraps of notepaper, that could not fail to touch the heart of anyone who read them, as I was privileged to do to-day. With their gratefulness to New South Wales, they linked their thanks to the Princess with whom they all seemed now to have some bond in common.

" We hope the new little Prince will enjoy all the health and happiness we wish our own little boy,"̤ wrote one woman. " My husband and I wish Princess Elizabeth

Photo: Sport & General

Drawing for the cot blankets.

The births registered in England, Scotland, Wales and Northern Ireland on the day that he was born numbered 2,272. This figure was obtained by that great and happy organization, the Women's Voluntary Services, when they were carrying out a draw for two hundred pairs of cot blankets, presented by the people of New South Wales, in far-away Australia, to babies born in Britain on Prince Charles's birthday. Princess Elizabeth herself helped to draw the winners' names from the lucky-dip box. When the W.V.S. informed the lucky ones of their good fortune, there came pouring

the great joy in her baby which we are finding in ours," ran another letter. This was the twelfth child for one mother who had been lucky in the draw. Another had had twin girls on November 14.

Meanwhile, the young Prince Charles, asleep in his pram, has been enjoying the warmth of the Spring sunshine in the Palace gardens ; as unconscious of all this public interest as of the assiduous photographer whose nursery pictures of him, paying earnest and fascinated attention to a toy rabbit or clutching his mother's pearl necklace, are now appearing in newspapers in most parts of the world. As with a lot of other babies, the camps are divided at the moment as to whether he is more like his mother than his father, or vice versa.

THURSDAY, APRIL 14, 1949. Old George Doggett, retired now from the Post Office where he had worked for thirty-two years, got up early and peered out of the bedroom window of the little three-roomed Council house at Shepherd's Bush to see what the day was like. It looked as though it would turn out fine, he thought, from the little he could see ; his eyes weren't very good now,

He had left everything ready overnight. so that there would be plenty of time in the morning. That was the best way when you lived alone and had to do everything for yourself. He had laid out his best black suit, a clean shirt and one of his best white collars and he had given his boots an extra polish. " Must look my best this morning," he muttered to himself as he dressed slowly and carefully. It was a pity about that old brown overcoat but it was the best he could do. Anyway, it was very warm and you needed warm clothes when you were nearly seventy. He went downstairs and had some tea and a bite to eat. Long before he needed to leave for Westminster Abbey, he had finished his small breakfast and was ready. He had looked forward to this day, Maundy Thursday, and to the service in the Abbey for so long. It was something to live for, from one year to another.

The little living room was spotlessly clean. There were only a few poor sticks of furniture but everything was neat and tidy. It had got very lonely in the last few years, living on his own, the old postman thought to himself. People always said London could be a very lonely place. He went once more round the room, to see that everything was in place ; he took a few shillings from the money on the window sill, where he always kept it, and then went over to the chest of drawers where his personal papers were tucked away among his shirts and collars. On the wall, just above his head, as he knelt searching was the testimonial the Post Office had given him when he had retired. He was very proud of the certificate and had had it framed.

Everything was filed tidily and he soon found the letter he wanted, the copy of the one he had written to the Bishop of Lichfield who was the Lord High Almoner. That was how it had all started, over two years before, with the writing of that letter. Slowly, he read it through again :

My Lord,

May I ask, please, if I may be considered for nomination for the Royal Maundy. I am sixty-six years of age and in receipt of the Old Age pension ; am partly blind and in straitened circumstances.

I was retired from the London postal service after thirty-two years unimpeachable service without pension on 1st March, 1940 on account of failing eyesight.

I descend from Thomas Doggett, the Drury Lane actor, who in the year 1715 founded Doggett's Coat and Badge in commemoration of the accession of H.M. King George I.

My grandfather, Robert Doggett, late Colour Sergeant, Coldstream Guards, of Garstang, Lancashire, was a pallbearer at the Duke of Wellington's funeral at St. Paul's Cathedral in 1852.

My father, Robert Francis Doggett, a well-known flautist of his time, had charge of the band on board H.M.S. Galatea *when H.R.H. Prince Alfred, Duke of Edinburgh, made his voyage round the world in the 'seventies.*

I should be most grateful for Your Lordship's kind consideration and would highly regard the honour, and if nominated would be able to attend the Abbey ceremony.

Any further particulars or testimonials Your Lordship may require will be furnished.

I am Your Lordship's humble servant,

George Albert Doggett.

The Bishop had thought his case a very suitable one and had sent the letter on to the Royal Almonry Office. Someone had died, causing a vacancy on the list, and so he had been appointed. As he had said in his letter, he regarded it as a great honour. He was very thankful, too, for the money which was now given in lieu of food and clothing. It worked out at £4. 15s. each year which was a great help. Though he had managed to save a little, all he had coming in now was the old age pension and 23s. 6d. a week blind welfare money.

Last year the King himself had come to the Abbey with the Queen to distribute the gifts but this year he would be unable to be present because he still had to take things quietly after his operation. Princess Elizabeth would be there, so he had read in his *The Times* (" My Bible " he called the paper ; he had taken it for years now) but she could not distribute the gifts on behalf of the King. Only the Lord High Almoner —the Bishop he had written to—could act for His Majesty in this.

He allowed himself plenty of time to get to the Abbey, catching a bus to Hammersmith Broadway and another one from there to Westminster. It was a sunny, pleasant morning and he was glad of that. The service started at noon but soon after eleven he went in through the great West door of the Abbey. Punctuality had grown into a habit during all those years with the Post Office.

He paused for a moment by the Unknown Warrior's tomb, noting the Flanders poppies and the tall candles there. 1914-18. It all seemed so very long ago now, dim in memory. It was two years before the war that his wife had died. He walked down one of the side aisles—over the worn, uneven stones, past the monuments and the memorials—and they showed him to where he was to sit, just in front of the choir stalls. The Abbey seemed so calm and restful after the rush of the London streets. He was glad to sit down. Some of the others were there already. Opposite him sat three old ladies in black. Each one of them, he thought, looked the very soul of respectability. Almost next to him was a man in a wheel chair. Leaning forward, bowed head resting in his hand, George Doggett murmured a short prayer under his breath.

On the back of the printed sheets giving the order of service was a short history of the Royal Maundy. His poor old eyes could just make it out. " The distribution of alms and the washing of the feet on the Thursday of Holy Week is of great antiquity," he read slowly. " The King's Maundy can be traced back in England with certainty to the twelfth century and there are continuous records of the distribution having been made on Maundy Thursday from the reign of King Edward I . . . From the beginning of the 15th century, the recipients have numbered as many old men and as many old women as the Sovereign is years of age." The service, it said, derived its name from the Latin word *mandatum*, meaning a commandment, and its opening words had always been : " A new Commandment have I given unto you, that ye love one another ; as I have loved you, that ye also love one another."

He had learnt a good deal about the service, one way and another, since he had gone on the list. It was all based on the teaching of the grace of humility. Even when the King himself made the distribution, he had to come down among them and hand them his gifts ; they didn't have to go up to him. The King was in his fifty-fourth year, so there would be fifty-four of them to receive the Maundy money this year. Those who were too old or too ill to come to the Abbey would have it sent to them.

Presently, the processions came, led by the Beadle of the Abbey bearing the Mace, behind which was carried the Cross of Westminster. The choirboys looked as innocent as angels, he thought to himself—

Photo: Daily Graphic

After the Royal Maundy service.   A handshake for the Dean of Westminster, Dr. Don.

but knew better than to imagine that they didn't get up to a bit of schoolboy mischief sometimes. Long ago, he had been a choir-boy himself.

Princess Elizabeth went past in the procession, walking beside the Dean. She passed so near him that he could have put out his hand and touched her. She was dressed all in blue and she was carrying a nosegay of sweet herbs. " She looks very much like her mother, the Queen," he thought.

Then came the procession of the Royal Almonry with the King's Bodyguard of the Yeomen of the Guard, all scarlet and gold, at the end of it. One of the Yeomen carried above his head the great silver Maundy dish on which were all the money purses. Old George Doggett, standing there in the choir,

watched them all go past him and wished only for one thing more—that the King could have been there.

The service started and he was soon wrapped and lost in the beauty of it all. He felt comforted and no longer lonely. " For He shall give His angels charge over thee," sang the fresh-faced choirboys and the sound of their young voices was as pure as a country dawn in the Spring-time.

There was the reading of a Lesson and then the Bishop made the first distribution. This was the clothing money, handed out from the great alms dish in coloured Tudor purses with long strings ; £1 15s. in a green purse to each woman and £2 5s. in a white purse to each man. The Bishop, he noticed, was wearing a white towel wrapped around him, like a plaid. Some of the others also wore towels. That was a reminder of the days when kings, in humility, washed the feet of the poor.

There was another Lesson, then the second distribution. This time the long-stringed purses were white and red. The white contained the small silver pennies, twopences, threepences and fourpences; fifty-four pence in all, because that was the King's age.

These little coins were specially minted at the Royal Mint. The red purses contained another £2 10s. for each man and woman.

The red and white purses disappeared into the worn black handbags of the old ladies standing there opposite George Doggett

and then the Lord High Almoner came round to him again. The Bishop smiled at him—a pleasant, friendly smile, it was—as he handed him the purses and the old postman gave him a hurried, unpractised bow, little more than just a quick bob up and down, as he took them. He put the two purses with the others in the pocket of his old brown overcoat.

Now the choir was singing again. The anthem rang through the Abbey.

Soon it was all over. George Doggett gave his little bow again as the Princess went past him, then joined the congregation slowly leaving. It was then that I spoke to him. "Something worth living for," he said. "Something to look forward to next year."

Photo: Baron

The Duchess of Kent with her children.

April 18 : The young Duke of Kent and his sister, Princess Alexandra on her pony, "Trustful". The Princess was competing in a gymkhana at Iver, Bucks., where the Duchess of Kent lives with her children.

WEDNESDAY, APRIL 20, 1949. Happiness came this afternoon to Victoria station, that busy, bustling railway terminus along the lengthy street from the Houses of Parliament.

It came smiling and laughing on the faces of fifty bright-eyed kiddies. A little shyly at first, it came ; and then, because it was so great a happiness, the shyness passed and the bright, smiling faces looked even happier than before. The uniformed porters who have never seemed a particularly happy race of men were cheered by its sunny influence and the railway officials,

unbending, became benign as favourite uncles.

The fifty children—pleasant little lads with hair trimmed and brilliantined for the occasion ; neat young girls in their new frocks and Sunday-best coats—were off on a month's holiday in Switzerland as the guests of the good people of Lucerne. Some of them had never had a real holiday before. Some were war orphans. All of them came from towns and cities that had been heavily bombed.

The city councillors and the hoteliers of Lucerne, whose own children had been

Photo : Keystone

British schoolchildren off on a month's holiday in Switzerland as the guests of the good people of Lucerne.

spared these horrors, had talked things over, wondering how they might best show their pleasure at the birth of a son to Princess Elizabeth. Some kindly heart had suggested this free holiday, with fares paid ; and so here were these children, setting off for the mountains and the clear lakeside.

Princess Elizabeth, driving round from Buckingham Palace, half a mile away, to see them off and to wish them a happy holiday, found them standing excitedly at the carriage doors of their train.

Large labels tied on to the jackets of the boys' neat new suits and on to the trim little coats of the girls had their names printed in capital letters together with the names of the hotels to which they were going. There was no danger of anyone getting lost.

They looked around them in wide-eyed wonderment—at the glistening Continental express, at the Press photographers and at the party of even more excited French boys and girls farther up the train. These French children were returning to Lille after a month's holiday in England, one of the many good works of the International Help the Children Fund. Some of them, too, were orphans of the war ; others the sons and daughters of Frenchmen who had been prisoners in the hands of the Germans. There will be many stories told in Lille, I think, of how they met the English Princess Elizabeth the day before her birthday and she spoke to them in French, asking all about their holiday.

"Hip Hip Hooray ! " shouted fifty young English voices as the train pulled out. " Vive la Princesse ! " cried the French boys and girls. They were all leaning out of the windows, waving and smiling, and the Princess stood on the platform waving back at them. It did one's heart good to see so much happiness and to think of the kindness of the councillors and hoteliers of Lucerne, waiting to receive them at the end of their journey.

THURSDAY, APRIL 21, 1949. " To-day is the anniversary of the birthday of Princess Elizabeth, Duchess of Edinburgh," So records that unique publication, the Court Circular, this evening.

How quickly the years pass ! Can it really be two years ago that one sat in Capetown at the end of the Royal tour of South Africa, listening to the twenty-one-years old Princess making her pledge to her father's peoples in many lands ? That was an historic broadcast : " I declare before you all that my whole life, whether it be long or short, shall be devoted to your service and the service of our great Imperial family to which we all belong. . . . God help me to make good my vow." Much has happened since then.

The battleship *Vanguard* sailed for England a few days later and every sea mile of the voyage was bringing the Princess nearer to the day when the King and Queen were to announce " the betrothal of their dearly beloved daughter, Princess Elizabeth, to Lieutenant Philip Mountbatten, R.N. . . . to which union, the King has gladly given his consent." That was in July. The wedding later that year was blessed with sunshine as welcome as it was unexpected on a November day in London.

The two years since the Capetown " twenty-first " celebrations have brought much personal happiness to the Princess. On her birthday to-day there were messages from many parts of the world to wish her well in the years to come. The Duke drove his wife up to London just after midday. They had spent the morning together with their baby son at Windlesham Moor, the country home outside Sunningdale which they leased soon after their marriage.

The King and Queen were giving a luncheon party for the Commonwealth Prime Ministers who are now conferring in London, so the birthday party became an Empire one.

MONDAY, APRIL 25, 1949. To-night the Queen took the two Princesses to the ballet at Covent Garden to see a fairy tale danced upon that vast stage. It had not been announced beforehand that Princess Elizabeth would attend this gala performance in aid of the Sadler's Wells Benevolent Fund. But who could resist the charm of Cinderella? The Princess, apparently, no more than the rest of us; and so she came with her mother and sister. Being there " unofficially," she did not occupy the flower-decked royal box with the Queen

the Opera House, the sombre buildings of Bow Street Police Court, seat of the chief metropolitan magistrate, were shut until the morning brought its fresh calendar of crime. Many a drama has been played out there.

If the hour was a little late for the dispensation of justice, it was a little early for the lamplighter. He came round soon after the ballet had begun, carrying his long pole on his shoulder, to light the gas lamps in the Covent Garden streets.

Inside, where red and white tulips decorated the royal box, a murmur of

The Queen and Princess Margaret at the Covent Garden ballet.

and Princess Margaret, but sat in another box nearby, out of the limelight.

The waiting crowds outside the Royal Opera House were rewarded by a brief glimpse of the Queen and the Princesses arriving. Just round the corner, the great vegetable and flower market that is Covent Garden's other claim to fame was for the moment closed but would be getting busy again at midnight. Across the road facing

admiration ran through the packed house when the Queen, magnificent in a crinoline-style dress and wearing a tiara of glittering diamonds, entered with Princess Margaret. Meanwhile Princess Elizabeth slipped quietly into her box.

Margot Fonteyn was dancing Cinderella. Ugly sisters, enchanting Cinderella, handsome Prince—no one enjoyed it all more than the two Princesses; not even the most enthusiastic of the young girls, far, far up in the topmost part of the gallery, almost in the roof.

THURSDAY, APRIL 28, 1949. To-day it was the turn of the people of North Wales to welcome Princess Elizabeth and the Duke of Edinburgh. At Bangor this morning, the Duke was installed as Chancellor of the University of Wales. The University sets great store by the personal relation which has always existed between the Royal House and itself. Princes of Wales have been, for the most part, the Duke's predecessors in office.

After his installation, there followed one of the most charming ceremonies of its kind that I have seen, when the Duke conferred the degree of Doctor of Music on his wife. They sat near one another on the platform in the college hall, the Duke wearing his magnificent black and gold robes over his naval uniform and the Princess in her scarlet and grey gown and mortar-board. The Vice-Chancellor, Principal Emrys Evans, presented the new graduate in words that were a Welsh poem :

" From a Welsh home across the narrow Straits sprang the House of Tudor and the first Elizabeth," he said. " A second Elizabeth we have in Her Majesty the Queen. Three things we pray for her daughter—the spacious times of the one

Photo: *The Times*

The Duke of Edinburgh as Chancellor of the University of Wales walks in procession with the Princess upon whom he conferred the degree of Doctor of Music.

Elizabeth, the gracious ways of the other ; and for herself, to have and to hand on to her son the kind heart and the simple faith. Of such three-fold grace may our Doctor of Music make for her precious life a splendid symphony through the musician's gift, that out of three sounds she frame, not a fourth sound, but a star."

The Vice-Chancellor led the Princess before her husband, who stood, tall above her, looking for the moment like some stern young headmaster receiving one of his pupils at a prizegiving. No pupil could have looked more demure or more impressed than the Princess as she looked up at him in his robes and his gold-tasselled mortar-board ; and then a little dimpled, querying smile flitted across her face as though she were saying to herself : " Imagine Philip being the Chancellor ! " There was a twinkle in the eye of the stern young headmaster as he acknowledged the presence of this young pupil by raising his mortar-board.

Now he looked a trifle doubtfully at the document in his hand. " Hawddamor Wraig dda," he said which, being translated, means " Welcome, good woman."

Photo: Liverpool Daily Post

" The Vice Chancellor led the Princess before her husband who stood, tall above her, looking for the moment like some stern young headmaster . . . "

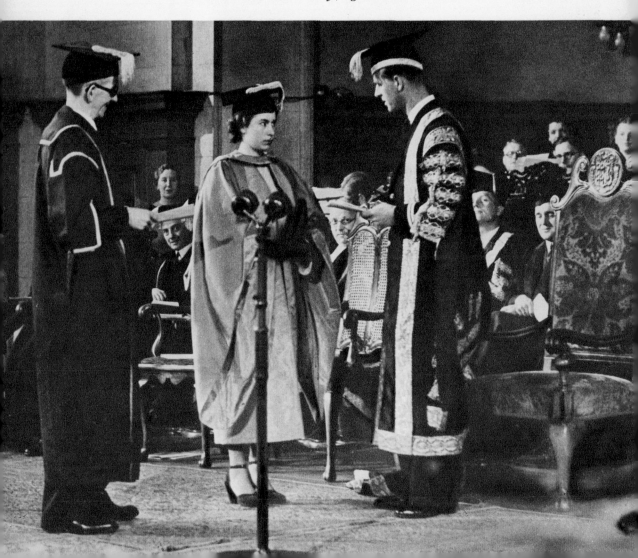

The Princess gazed a little in wonderment at this display of the Welsh tongue by her sailor-Chancellor husband, though no doubt she had heard some murmurings of his rehearsals. " Da gan y Llys dẏ dderbyn yn Ddoethur," continued the Duke, who is not the sort of man to be frightened by little difficulties of this sort. That meant : " The Court is pleased to receive you to the Doctorate." He gave the Princess-graduate a firm, full grip of the hand, for another of his qualities is that he does nothing half-heartedly ; and there they stood for a moment, smiling at one another, while the professors and the students and all the rest of the packed hall smiled with them, and filled the place with their applause.

Nine others received honorary degrees, including Mr. Attlee, the Prime Minister, the Archbishop of Wales (Dr. D. L. Prosser), Mr. Emlyn Williams, the Welsh playwright and actor, Lady Megan Lloyd George (" eminent among women in a Parliament of men," said the Vice-Chancellor), and the Rev. H. Elvet Lewis, the blind preacher-poet and former Archdruid of Wales.

The Duke had earlier made an interesting speech at his installation. " My generation, although reasonably well-schooled, is probably the worst educated of this age," he said. " The war cut short any chance there was of acquiring a higher education."

In the afternoon, sixteen hundred feet up on a mountain road, at the top of Crimea Pass, the Princess and the Duke passed out of Caernarvonshire and into the county of Merioneth. Not for a great many years had the style and title Earl of Merioneth been held in Wales until the King conferred the Earldom upon his son-in-law as his second title. Now, for the first time, Merionethshire displayed her beauties of mountain and valley in the early summer sunshine to her Earl and Countess who had come to meet the people of the towns and the countryside. High up on the galleries of the slate quarries at Blaenau Festiniog they fired 3,500 sticks of gelignite in a quarrymen's Royal salute. It sounded like flak in wartime.

Photo : Y Cymro

A roadside welcome, amid the mountains, to Merionethshire.

FRIDAY, APRIL 29, 1949. The grim grey walls of Harlech's fighting castle, scene of many a bloody fight, echoed to-day to the tune of the harp and the sound of children's voices singing. The Princess's Standard flew with the Four Lion Standard of Wales above the ancient battlements. A keen wind swept the ruins which stand, dominating, above the waters of Cardigan Bay. The people of Harlech gathered within the inner ward of the old fortress to welcome the Princess and the Duke whose visit will add another line or two to its centuries-old story. Children's voices raised the old battle song, " March of the Men of Harlech." The sound of their singing went echoing through the castle, startling the ravens, and was lost on the wind that carried it out towards the sea.

A quarryman-poet from Blaenau Festiniog had composed verses of welcome and they were sung by the harpist in the Welsh tongue. Translated, the last verse ran :

*We wish you could stay and make Wales your
    home,*
Our castles are vacant, and so is our throne.
Do linger awhile till our language you'll learn,
And to your young son, you can teach it in turn.
*Our joy would be echoed o'er mountains and
    dales*
To see baby Charles a Welsh Prince of Wales.

The Princess and the Duke met and chatted with many of the local people, as

Photo: Y Cymro

" *The grim grey walls of Harlech's fighting castle, scene of many a bloody fight . . .* "

they do everywhere they go. Then they drove on through lovely Merionethshire to the county town of Dolgelley. People turned out all along the road to greet them.

There is a great and sincere quality of friendliness about the Princess and the Duke. We had an instance of it on this drive. They were running twenty minutes ahead of time as they approached Dolgelley, so they stopped along the roadside and got out of their car to admire the view across to the Cader range of mountains, mist-capped in the distance. Walking down the road, hoping for no more than a glimpse of the Princess and the Duke as they drove past, came an elderly couple, seeking a good spot to stand and wait. Rounding a

bend in the road, they found themselves suddenly face to face with the King's daughter and her husband. The Duke strolled over to them as though they were old friends. The Princess followed. Soon the man was pointing out local landmarks and chatting about gardening and painting and fishing while his wife was asking after Prince Charles. The four of them stood there talking in the middle of the road for about ten minutes.

At Dolgelley, there was another ceremony of welcome in the crowded town square. " The memory of everything that we have seen and heard to-day will not fade quickly from our minds," said Merioneth's Earl, " and we shall always look forward to the day we can come back."

Photo: The Times

April 28 : The first Royal Academy dinner to be held for ten years. The Duke of Gloucester is seen replying to the toast of the King and the Royal Family. Among those at the top table (reading from left to right) are : Mr. P. Noel Baker, The Earl of Athlone, the Archbishop of Canterbury, the Duke of Gloucester, Sir Alfred Munnings, the Turkish Ambassador and Mr. Winston Churchill.

SOME MAY VIGNETTES

WEDNESDAY, MAY 11, 1949. The diary for the last ten days or so illustrates very well the wide variety of engagements that members of the Royal Family undertake. On the day following their Welsh tour, Princess Elizabeth and the Duke of Edinburgh with the Duke of Gloucester were at the Football Association Cup Final. A Wembley crowd of 100,000 saw Wolverhampton Wanderers beat Leicester City 3—1 and watched the Princess present the cup to the captain of the winning team. Twenty-four hours later, on the Sunday, the scene changed to the quadrangle of Windsor Castle where Boy Scouts attending the National Scouts' service in St. George's

Photo: International News

The Duke of Edinburgh shaking hands with the players at the F.A. Cup Final.

Photo: Graphic Photo Union

A parade of Boy Scouts at Windsor Castle.

Chapel marched past the Princess and her husband. On the Monday, there was a Royal visit to the British Industries Fair at Earl's Court, where Queen Mary, who has never missed the Fair since it started, spent two hours and fifty minutes touring the exhibition with the Queen, Princess Elizabeth, the Duke of Edinburgh and the Princess Royal. That evening, the King and Queen gave a party at the Palace for the Foreign Ministers attending the London conference on the Council of Europe ; the

Duke of Edinburgh went to the annual dinner of the Newspaper Society.

The wide range continues : The Queen and Princess Elizabeth at an Albert Hall performance of " Hiawatha " in aid of the Battersea Central Mission ; Princess Elizabeth and the Duke visiting the Stock Exchange ; the Duke at the annual dinner of the Marylebone Cricket Club at Lord's ; another visit to the B.I.F., this time to the Olympia section ; Princess Elizabeth at a charity matinee ; the Duke of Edinburgh addressing a great international Youth Forum at the Albert Hall with Mr. Attlee, the Prime Minister, and Mr. Anthony Eden as fellow speakers. Meanwhile, the King worked at his desk. Queen Mary and the Princess Royal, the Duke and Duchess of Gloucester and the Duchess of Kent, too,

she is Patron. Her husband, having visited the Honourable Company of Master Mariners on board their headquarters ship, Wellington, anchored off the Thames Embankment, drove out to Notting Hill to visit yet another boys' club.

Photo: Photographic News

May 10 : An incident during the visit of Princess Elizabeth and the Duke of Edinburgh to the British Industries Fair at Birmingham.

went about their manifold engagements.

To-day, after addressing the National Federation of Young Farmers, the Princess went on to a reception held by the Linen and Woollen Drapers Institution, of which

THURSDAY, MAY 12, 1949. Windsor Horse Show is a pure delight on a sunny summer's day such as we have had to-day. They hold it each year in the meadows of the Home Park, below the castle, towards Eton.

One could not wish for a more impressive and lovely setting than this. The chestnut trees in the park were in fine full bloom, the turf was sprinkled white with daisies. Here the Thames flows peacefully through the meadows, carrying only pleasure steamers and languid punts, holiday boating parties and energetic rowing crews. Windsor Castle towers above everything, reminding

for the day. There were deck chairs set out in the sunshine facing the ring, where the hunters and the ponies were put through their paces from ten in the morning till early evening. There was luncheon in marquees.

The troopers of the Life Guards and the Royal Horse Guards, riding down from their barracks in the town to the park,

Photo: Planet News

Presenting a prize at the Royal Windsor Horse Show. The castle forms the background to the scene.

all who pass through the busy entrance gates that this is a Royal show and has the King for Patron.

It was pleasant to get away from noisy London and into this country atmosphere

treated the mundane motor traffic with magnificent disdain. As they passed along the Datchet road below the Castle, one pictured them riding to the joust; the coats of their black chargers a glossy sheen, their helmet plumes tossing and their pennanted lances carried high.

Princess Elizabeth who has always been extremely keen on riding and horse-racing —and, indeed, anything at all to do with horses—arrived with the Duke just before lunch and remained until nearly four o'clock. The Duke, recently elected the new President of that great power in the world of cricket, the Marylebone Cricket Club, was wearing his M.C.C. tie. Princess Elizabeth presented some of the prizes and perhaps remembered when as a young girl she, too, was a competitor and prize-winner at the show.

The day passed pleasantly and gently. One of the big events was the musical ride by the troopers of the Household Cavalry. Even the aproned caterer's cooks and washers-up came out of their tented kitchens to look at this spectacle.

Photo: P.A.-Reuter

May 19 : Queen Mary, patroness of Bedford College for Women (University of London) since 1913, attends the Assembly and garden party held in Regent's Park, London. The College is celebrating its centenary.

FRIDAY, MAY 20, 1949. This past week has been notable in that it has seen the King carrying out his first large-scale engagements since the operation just over two months ago. On Wednesday, and again yesterday, Their Majesties held an afternoon presentation party indoors at the Palace. There were about two thousand guests on each occasion.

These presentation parties take the place of the more formal and more spectacular courts of pre-war memory. For the young debutantes who are invited, attendance in itself is regarded officially as presentation at Court. So, though they may sigh for the magnificent evening functions that marked their mothers' presentations, the honour that is done them is no less than it was in those more expansive days. Court feathers and fans and elaborate Court gowns are deemed not to fit in with this austere era. One wonders whether they will ever return?

Impatient in the car queue in the Mall, some of Wednesday's young debutantes got out and went stepping gingerly up the footway, carefully avoiding the rain puddles. The crowd outside the gates viewed the ingoing fashions with a critical eye.

The guests gathered in the State drawing rooms, in the long picture gallery and the State ballroom. It was easy to pick out the debutantes in their colourful silk frocks and their dainty summer hats, trimmed with flowers and veiling. They looked as demure as bridesmaids, for all their excitement.

Around the room could be heard all the accents of the Empire. In this colourful scene, the saris of the Indian women stood out in gold and blue and white. The tall, soldierly officers of the Honourable Corps of Gentlemen-at-Arms, standing guard with hands on their sword hilts, looked every inch as romantic as Dumas' Musketeers.

The deep curtseys went undulating like a wave through the ballroom as the King, who was in the uniform of Admiral of the Fleet, entered with the Queen. The men bowed. One heard many comments that the King looked rested and well. Their Majesties took seats in the ballroom for the formal presentation of members of the Diplomatic Corps and their wives, then passed slowly through the various rooms among the guests. Here and there, some young girl—more fortunate than the others —would be presented personally. The pre-war procedure, of course, was that each one passed before the King and Queen to make her curtsey.

Their Majesties stayed an hour on Wednesday and an hour and three-quarters on the following day, when the second party was held. That in itself may be taken as a measure of the improvement the King has made.

MONDAY, MAY 23, 1949 A Royal visit to Lord's is usually reckoned to be worth a quick wicket to the fielding side, the experts there like to tell you. Events and two stout-hearted New Zealand batsmen proved them wrong to-day. The New Zealanders were playing M.C.C., who included the England captain, F. G. Mann, the dynamic Edrich and that hero of all the autograph-hunting schoolboys, Denis Compton, who was celebrating his birthday.

The King arrived during the afternoon's play, driving in through the Grace memorial gates with the Queen and entering the august pavilion through a quiet doorway of that holy of holies. The New Zealanders had had a bad morning and six wickets had fallen for only 94 runs in reply to a useful total of 379 by M.C.C. The King and Queen, watching the game from the sacrosanct committee room, saw the tourists' total steadily raised by Messrs. Mooney and Rabone, numbers seven and eight in the batting order.

In the Long Room of the pavilion, across the passageway from the committee room,

Princess Margaret walks in procession at the Vatican, on her way to be received by the Pope in private audience.

Photo: Planet News

PRINCESS MARGARET IN ITALY

Princess Margaret spent the month of May in Italy, Switzerland and Paris. It was her first Continental holiday. The Princess flew home from Paris on June 1, thrilled by all she had seen during her four weeks tour. In the three countries she visited, she left delightful memories of her charm and friendliness.

As does everyone who goes to Venice, the Princess went down the Grand Canal in a gondola.

Photo: Keystone

Left : Following her audience with the Pope, the Princess was shown some of the treasures of the Vatican, saw also the Sistine Chapel and the great Church of St. Peter.

Photo: Planet News

The Director of the British School of Archaeology in Rome, Professor Ward Perkins, points out to the Princess features of interest during a visit to the Forum.

Photo: Associated Press

the members sat on their high stools looking out through the windows, intent on the game and full of cricket wisdom. Cricket memories over many years are enshrined in this place. The bearded Grace in his small-peaked, ringed cap looks down on the modern scene from one of the paintings on the walls. There are old and mellow pictures of games played long ago on English village greens. In these, the thatched cottages nestle cosily among the trees under which ancient gaffers sit puffing at their pipes; there are donkeys grazing on the boundary and there are ducks on the nearby pond. The inscription on one such painting runs:

"Match between Rochester C.C. and the Gentlemen and servants of the Darnley Estate, played on the estate near Cobham Hall. Charles Dickens of Gads Hill takes the score. August 2nd 1867."

The eminent scorer appears to have a tall and refreshing glass in front of him as he sits, top-hatted, in the shade of a tree.

Another picture, in which the braces of the players are much in evidence, depicts a scene at Lord's in 1837 when there was a match to commemorate the first fifty years of the Marylebone Cricket Club. With the exception of a church, now hidden by a block of flats, none of the buildings portrayed in 1837 remains.

There are some old bats, all of them dark brown and one of them almost black, to tell the story of the evolution of the bat between the years 1770 and 1800. Nearby, along the wall, you will find one of the great Sir Donald Bradman's unmerciful bats. There, also, you may see what the old two-stump wicket in use prior to 1775 looked like. There is a stuffed sparrow in a glass case close by one of the fireplaces. "This sparrow was killed at Lord's by a ball bowled by Jehangir Khan (Cambridge) to T. N. Pearce (M.C.C.), July 3rd, 1936," says the label.

In the bar behind the Long Room, where you may also obtain tea and buns, the wall is covered with pictures of teams, ancient and modern. Here are to be found the old stalwarts who did battle against Australia long ago and their successors down the years. Here, too, is an interesting score card of a match between the Gentlemen of Norfolk and I Zingari, played at Sandringham on two July days in the year 1866. His Royal Highness the Prince of Wales, opening the innings for I.Z., was bowled by a Norfolk gentleman named Wright before he had scored. The Royal "duck" is recorded for all to see. The Prince did not have the opportunity of another knock, for his side won by an innings and 98 runs. Photographs of the players—some reclining elegantly on the Sandringham turf, others looking most comfortable in deep wicker arm-chairs and nearly all of them wearing mutton-chop side-whiskers—incline one to imagine that this must have been a most amiable and hospitable match.

The New Zealanders, Messrs. Mooney and Rabone, were for the moment more concerned with the problems of the immediate present, including that of the new ball which they had shortly to face, than with recollections of the past. They remained and the score mounted towards respectability. After the tea interval, still not out, they lined up with the rest of their team-mates and the M.C.C. players in front of the pavilion. The decorous claps of the members were lost in the great welcome that the stands and the ringside gave the King and Queen as they came out to meet the players of both teams and to welcome the New Zealanders to this country. This was the King's first public appearance since his illness. The big crowd showed how pleased they were to see His Majesty about again. It was the sort of reception that Lord's reserves for one of its favourites when he reaches his double century.

Out on the field, the King and Queen chatted with all the players, then returned to the pavilion to see more of the game.

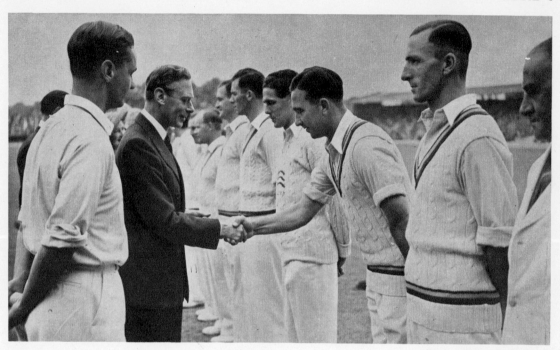

Photo: *Sport & General*

Going down the line of M.C.C. cricketers, the King shakes hands with Denis Compton, hero of all the autograph-hunting schoolboys.

Now for the Royal quick wicket, said the experts, sitting up expectantly. This was the moment when excitement should overcome batsmanship. But Messrs. Mooney and Rabone, refusing to lend proof to the legend, proceeded to put on a great many more runs. They were still together when the hands of the clock crept round to six-thirty, bringing another day's cricket at Lord's to its close in evening sunshine.

There is another legend that you may hear at Lord's, though I will not vouch for the truth of this one any more than the New Zealand batsmen would comply with the terms of the other. An old member, much respected for his years, waking from his afternoon's dreams of cricket, saw ladies in the pavilion (so the story runs). "Ladies?" muttered the old member. "Ladies in the Long Room at Lords? Unheard of. Quite unheard of. Must write to *The Times* about it."

"It's Her Majesty the Queen," they told him. "Her Majesty the Queen and her lady-in-waiting."

"Different matter altogether," said the old member. "Altogether a different matter. A great honour. Very great honour indeed."

It was some minutes later that the afterthought occurred to him. "You can assure me, of course," he said, "that this is not the thin end of the wedge?"

TUESDAY, MAY 24, 1949. Once again, now that the war is over, there blossoms and blooms again in the springtime the Chelsea Flower Show, an event which is the joy of all gardeners—and the despair of a good many of the amateur ones.

Before the eyes of the bemedalled, red-coated Chelsea Pensioners—well accustomed to this annual transformation of their

Hospital grounds—there appear cool, enchanting rock gardens, where only a little while before was just a grassy slope. Old-world gardens are made with new-world rapidity. Great marquees, spreading over nearly three acres of ground, are filled with the colour and beauty of the flowers, each one a challenge to the others in delicacy and fragrance and loveliness. There are vegetables, too ; vegetables so perfect, so spotless and so artistically arranged that for the moment one is persuaded that carrots are grown, not to be eaten but just to be looked at.

All this, it is interesting to reflect, had its beginnings one day in March in the year 1804 when a few gentlemen, sitting round a table in the premises of Mr. Hatchard, publisher, in Piccadilly, decided to form a society " to collect every information respecting the cultivation of plants and trees " and " to foster and encourage every branch of horticulture." Mr. John Wedgwood, of pottery fame, presided at the meeting and the new organization, thus founded, was named the Horticultural Society of London. It was in 1861, when the Prince Consort was President, that a new Charter granted it the title of " The Royal Horticultural Society." To-day, the Society has a membership of approximately 35,000 and there are some 1,400 Horticultural Societies affiliated to it.

The Queen, visiting the Show this morning, found it back again to pre-war standards of quality and size and saw it at its freshest and best, before the gates were open. While the judges were still going round with their notebooks and pencils, Lord Aberconway, the President, escorted Her Majesty on a tour of the grounds. She paused longest of all, perhaps, to admire the blue perfection of the delphiniums. No one among all the many thousands of visitors who will follow before the Show closes on Friday will find more real pleasure in it.

Apropos of Royal visits, Lord Aberconway told an amusing story at lunch. " A member of the Royal Family was honouring us with a visit one year," he said, " and the customary number of photographers awaited his arrival. He stepped from his car to find them poised, ready for action. Left and right, the cameras clicked. The Royal visitor was not without a sense of humour. ' Last night, at ten o'clock, fulfilling a public engagement in London, I was photographed by twenty photographers, complete with all the paraphernalia of flashlamps,' he said. ' This morning, not more than twelve hours later, they photograph me again. Yet I am not aware that my appearance has changed unduly during the night ! ' "

WEDNESDAY, MAY 25, 1949. In the green, sheltered garden of Buckingham Palace, the officers, non-commissioned officers and guardsmen of the First Battalion, the Welsh Regiment of Foot Guards saw their old Colours borne proudly before them. The rich colourings—the crimson, the gold, the blue and the white—were faded now after nearly a quarter of a century, though the battle honours still stood out plainly for all to see.

For the last time, the Battalion saluted its old Colours. Softly, the notes gradually dying away, the band played " Auld Lang Syne " as the two brave standards were marched off parade. Their years of service were ended.

Now the King, in full-dress uniform, came out of the Palace to present the new Colours that rested, for the moment, on piled drums.

" Reverend Sir," said the Commanding Officer, addressing the Chaplain when the King had made his inspection. " On behalf of the Regiment, we ask you to bid God's blessing on these Colours."

" We are ready so to do," came the

Photo: Photographic News

" On bended knee, the two Second Lieutenants detailed as officers for the Colours received them from the King . . . "

Chaplain's reply. He paused for a moment. Then he spoke again. " We are gathered here to consecrate these Colours, the solemn symbols of our loyalty, and with them ourselves, our service and our life," he said. " May they never be unfurled save in the cause of justice, righteousness and truth."

" Let us pray," he said. The voices of the tall guardsmen, making the responses, were a low murmur through the ranks. Then, laying his hand on the Colours, the Chaplain consecrated them. " In the faith of Jesus Christ and to the glory of God," were the words he used.

The Lord's Prayer was said. There was a prayer for all past and present members of the Regiment of Welsh Guards.

On bended knee, the two Second Lieutenants detailed as officers for the Colours received them from the King, Colonel-in-Chief of the Regiment, who now addressed the battalion.

" When my father, King George the Fifth, presented your old Colours which you have just saluted for the last time," he said, " the war of 1914 was still uppermost in men's thoughts. Your Regiment had only recently been born ; your battalion had already learnt to endure and to overcome the dangers and miseries of war.

" Since that day at Windsor nearly twenty-five years ago, you have seen hard service in many lands and I know that my father, who took so deep an interest in the formation of the Welsh Guards, would have found the greatest pride and satisfaction in your record."

The guardsmen, stiff at attention, listened intently to every word.

" Though you visited Egypt in peace, war was already inevitable when in 1939 you were sent to garrison the Rock of Gibraltar. You returned to France and in the fighting which followed in the spring of 1940 your share was a full one. Once more in Normandy and the Low Countries, as a part of the Guards Armoured Division, you assisted in long and bitter fighting to reverse the decision of Dunkirk. Since then you have served in Palestine, and there again you have shown, by discipline and forbearance, how fully you deserve the trust which has so often been placed in you. . . . I hand these new Colours to you in full confidence that you will guard them well ; and that in peace or war, whatever the future may bring, you will keep bright the honour of the Welsh Guards and of Wales."

The sun shone bright on the Colours as the battalion marched back to barracks.

THURSDAY, MAY 26, 1949. At one minute before twelve o'clock on a May night eighty-two years ago, a Princess was born in Kensington Palace. Her parents were the young, handsome Duke of Teck and his friendly, popular Duchess, Princess Mary Adelaide, favourite cousin of Queen Victoria. Eight names were chosen for the child. She was christened Victoria Mary Augusta Louisa Olga Pauline Claudine Agnes. But they called her May, after the lovely month in which she had been born. The world knows her now as Queen Mary, the heart of the Royal Family circle.

To-day was Queen Mary's birthday and from many parts of the world there poured into Marlborough House, her London home just off Pall Mall, messages of congratulation and good wishes.

She looks out from Marlborough House on to a very different world from that in which she was brought up. But, while many orders change, Queen Mary remains the same gracious lady—rolled parasol and toque unaltering—who long ago won a nation's esteem and warm-hearted affection.

At eighty-two, she finds life full of interest. The days never pall or flag. She keeps closely in touch still with the many good causes that have had her staunch support and generous encouragement through the years. Hospital visits, the helping of the sick and the poor, occupy much of her time, as they always have done. She supervises the running of her household with such minute exactitude that she has her finger on everything, whether it be a question of the housekeeping bills, a new

flower bed in the gardens, the arrangements in the kitchens or the spring-cleaning of the rooms. Nothing misses the eagle eye of Queen Mary in her own home—or anywhere else, for that matter. She runs her house with kindly firmness.

She rises early, invariably breakfasts alone in her private suite of rooms overlooking the Mall and, at ten-thirty, summons her lady-in-waiting and her private secretary to deal with her correspondence and such other matters as may need attention.

The afternoon is Queen Mary's customary time for visiting. She prefers nowadays to make informal, private visits to the various institutions in which she is interested, rather than to have a great deal of fuss and formality. Often, of an afternoon, she will go out for a drive, particularly at this time of the year. It may be, perhaps, to Windsor or round one of the London parks or down to Kew Gardens to see the flowers. Another day, Queen Mary may decide on a visit to one of the art galleries ; she sees every new and worth-while London exhibition.

Whatever the programme is, it is carried out with remarkable thoroughness. At the hospitals, Queen Mary looks into every nook and cranny. Every painting comes under close scrutiny at the art galleries. And, when recently she went to a private dress show at one of the great London fashion houses, she asked—having seen the fashions—if she might go round the workrooms.

Queen Mary's visits to the British Industries Fair have already become legendary. The Duke of Gloucester once said : " I think my mother has walked most people off their feet at the Fair." Many of the officials who have accompanied her on her tours are not inclined to disagree with that statement. Even to-day, she will make a two-and-a-half hours tour, vividly interested all the time in everything she sees and asking all sorts of questions.

She wastes no waking hour. Even on

Photo: Daily Graphic

May 21 : A few days before her eighty-second birthday, Queen Mary opens a new block of flats for aged people in Islington.

some of her car drives, Queen Mary will have her lady-in-waiting read to her from the newspaper.

Antiques and the theatre are two of Queen Mary's great interests. At the theatre, the leading players are invariably asked to the royal box during the interval, so that she can have a chat with them about the play and their parts. Her favourites, not unnaturally, are mostly to be found among the theatrical " old-timers." She seems to prefer domestic comedies but puts no ban on a good thriller if one is recommended to her. More occasionally, she goes to the cinema—but much prefers the theatre.

As for antiques, wherever they may be found, they are an irresistible attraction. Long experience has made Queen Mary an expert judge of pieces. Marlborough House is full of beautiful things of a past age. Queen Mary—cataloguing them in her clear handwriting, displaying them in the gracious rooms and handling the lovely jade—treasures them as a connoisseur. Her collection, gathered searchingly over many years, is one of the finest in London.

She used to spend many hours gardening. At one time, whenever she went for a holiday to Sandringham or Balmoral, she would take her own set of gardening tools with her. She clipped hedges as energetically as she toured the B.I.F. Though she does little in the garden now, she can still be stirred into action at the sight of ivy. Queen Mary hates ivy as deeply as she loves antiques. Not a suspicion of it is allowed to grow anywhere at Marlborough House. And, coming across it elsewhere, she has sometimes been known to give it a fierce little jab with her rolled parasol.

Queen Mary is present at every big occasion at Buckingham Palace. Garden parties, dinners to distinguished visitors, luncheons to Empire Prime Ministers—whatever the function is, her presence adds interest to it. Her health remains good, her eyesight and hearing are excellent. She has troubled the doctors but seldom, even in recent years.

She is often at the Palace, too, for little family gatherings with the King and Queen ; for lunch or tea. To-day, there was a luncheon party there to celebrate her birthday. One of her greatest joys within the family now is to watch her great-grandson, Prince Charles of Edinburgh, growing up. Queen Mary is a frequent visitor to his nursery.

Sunday morning is set aside, without fail, for church. She usually goes to Westminster Abbey or to St. Michael's, set in the quiet of Chester Square, joining in the service with the other members of the congregation.

Always, Queen Mary's motto has been Service for others. She has had her full share of sorrow and anxiety. But at eighty-two—surrounded by her family, loved by everybody—she is thoroughly enjoying her old age.

SATURDAY, MAY 28, 1949. Belfast is a city where Irish hearts beat most loyal to the British Throne. But in the South, where the new Republic of Eire was recently proclaimed, things are different. Political tension between North and South, raising its head recently, had led to un-official suggestions that the visit of Princess Elizabeth and her husband to the northern city of Belfast might be postponed. On Wednesday afternoon, however, they landed at the Royal Air Force aerodrome at Aldergrove to carry out their programme as it had originally been planned. Neither of them was in the least bit likely to be deterred from doing so. This evening, when they were flying home again, the Governor of Northern Ireland, Vice-Admiral the Earl Granville, sent this telegram to the King at Buckingham Palace :

" *With my humble duty to your Majesty, I have the honour to inform you that Their Royal Highnesses the Princess Elizabeth, Duchess of Edinburgh, and the Duke of Edinburgh left Ulster to-day after a most successful visit. They charmed everyone and were received everywhere by all classes with unbounded enthusiasm and loyalty. The speech of Her Royal Highness at the City Hall, Belfast, should give a spiritual uplift to the whole country. We pray before long we may see them again.*"

The Governor's telegram was a good summing up.

Nothing could have pleased the Ulster people more, declared one of the Belfast papers, than the Princess's words when she and the Duke received the Freedom of the City on Thursday morning. " Crossing the seas, even in an aeroplane, usually makes people feel that they are going far from home," she said ; " but when Belfast is at the end of the journey, that feeling is only an illusion. The warmth of an Irish welcome, the loyalty which the very name of Ulster recalls, the sight of your great factories and shipyards—all these, in different ways, remove any thought of separation, and make us feel as much at home in your midst as in any other part of the United Kingdom." It was a delicate tribute, particularly at this moment.

The speech, delivered amid all the impressive ceremonial that civic dignity employs on these occasions, was one of the most outstanding I have heard the Princess make. It had in it the regal ring. Here, said those who listened, was a future Queen, making pronouncement, and they were left in no doubt of the Princess's qualities of mind and strength of character.

She spoke of the kindness with which she and her husband had been received from the day of their marriage, wherever they had been. " It will be hard for us to be worthy of so much affection," she said ; " but we know that it springs largely from the fact that the Crown is the focus of our unity, comradeship and moral standards. We shall spare no effort to promote those ends which, however times may change, are themselves unchangeable. I do not think we can do better than try to follow the example set by my parents and grand-parents."

Now the Princess touched upon a wider scene. " Although small in territory, the United Kingdom has a great history," she declared. " The exploits of its people, English, Scottish, Irish, and Welsh—so different in origin and so well blended in the whole—have left their stamp on the world, even deeper than that of the Roman Empire.

" Our strength, founded on our unity and fostered by the industry of great towns such as this, is neither aggressive nor exclusive. We have never yielded to force, but our aim is to maintain our influence through good-will among the nations, rather than in empty appearance of power and domination. Whatever our failings, this is one virtue that men and women of our stock have carried to every continent. I believe that in this divided world, the British Commonwealth is one of the most wholesome influences that exists. Its members, like those of many families, may disagree. They may take different sides in questions at issue. They do not all have the same law, language or even coinage. Their worth and ideals rise

above those things and their power for good is all the greater because they have never been the slaves of uniformity."

Whispered an Irishman : " She sounds a young woman who'd stand for no sort of nonsense at all, so she does."

" These are days when men's consciences are uneasy," went on the Princess and her young voice was very firm. " In fifty years, the world has seen greater changes than in the preceding five hundred, and much that seemed built on rock has shifted as if the foundation were sand. Yet beneath the sand is one solid layer which nothing has been able to break. I am sure that what is best in our countrymen comes from the habits and the wisdom bred in them by centuries of Christianity. We may be living on the moral capital which past generations have built up. Traditions which have no living basis soon become meaningless, and our children will suffer if we have no more to offer them than the virtues which we ourselves owe to an age of greater faith.

" It would be our greatest service to mankind if the British peoples, who set the standard of law and justice for many countries, and who are now leading the world in the establishment of social security, should also be the pioneers of a moral and spiritual revival without which all our great and material achievements would have been in vain."

There is no doubt that the Princess's speech created a profound impression and carried far beyond the walls of Belfast's City Hall in which it was delivered. In the crowded streets, she and the Duke were welcomed tumultuously as they drove through the city.

At the luncheon which followed every-body's Irish fancy was tickled by the neat-ness of the Duke's humour when he replied on behalf of the Princess and himself to the Lord Mayor's toast of " Our youngest Burgesses." " We went to the British Industries Fair the other day," he said,

" and we were presented with a whole lot of pillow cases for our son. It may be some small consolation to you to know that although he is not here on Irish soil, his head is resting on Irish linen."

In the afternoon, at Queen's Island, the two Royal visitors saw something of Belfast's great industries.

At night, the Government gave a State banquet in the Central Hall of Parliament Buildings. The Princess, in her white, full-skirted picture frock, embroidered in crystal beading, has never looked lovelier. Diamonds glittered in her tiara and necklace and in the heavy bracelet on her right wrist, over her elbow-length glove. The riband of the Order of the Garter slashed a vivid kingfisher blue across the bodice of the dress. The Prime Minister, Sir Basil Brooke, escorted the Princess in to dinner, the Duke following.

After this glittering overnight scene, the drive the following morning through Sandy Row, one of Belfast's working-class streets, added point to the city's great welcome. On these Royal visits up and down the country it is often the case that the poorer the district, the greater the welcome. Sandy Row, which is so Royal that they have even named one of its " pubs " Royal Bar, was a case in point. You could hardly see the street for all the flags and pennants and bunting. The crowds were tremendous —and deafening. The Princess and the Duke, one imagines, will long remember Sandy Row and the manner in which they were received as they drove slowly down the street on this day in May. The people of the Row, with thousands more from the neighbouring streets adding to their numbers, really let themselves go.

As on the first day, there was a visit to a linen warehouse—this one at the end of Sandy Row—where some of the women workers expressed their feelings by turning out in Union Jack overalls. In the afternoon, the presence of the Princess and the Duke at the Royal Ulster Agricultural Society's show at Balmoral attracted an attendance which set up a new record in the eighty-two years history of this event.

SUNDAY, MAY 29, 1949. The silent car that came slowly up Constitution Hill, running parallel with the spike-topped garden wall of Buckingham Palace, carried a smiling young lady dressed in blue. It was a blue in one of those delicate shades that puzzle the average man to describe faithfully, being darkish, yet not truly dark blue ; nor was it a royal blue or a sapphire blue, proclaimed those who know about these matters. Whatever the exact shade was, it looked very becoming upon the young lady who wore it.

At this hour on a Sunday morning, there are usually but few people to be found hereabouts. But to-day, they lined the Hill, which is really no more than the gentlest of slopes, from the Palace to the gates up at Hyde Park corner. The day was sunlit and the shadows of the fresh-leafed trees on the palace side and on the park side opposite almost met in the centre of the well-paved roadway. At the last minute, more people came running across Green Park to wave to the young lady as she drove by. All the comfortable deck chairs set out on the grass were left empty in the sunshine.

As the car drove on, eighty trumpeters sounded a fanfare that went echoing eastwards across to Piccadilly and westwards to Knightsbridge. To the north, they heard the challenge of it beyond Marble Arch and southwards it reached the Thames.

At the top of Constitution Hill, at Hyde Park Corner, stands a noble memorial to officers and men of the Royal Artillery who died in the first world war. It is set on an island amid a sea of London traffic. The great howitzer, carved in stone and mounted on a massive plinth which places it high above the street, is a London landmark. Standing below their gun, the bronze figures of the artillerymen around the plinth are grim and sure upholders of the motto of the regiment : Wherever Fame and Glory Lead.

The young lady in blue, stepping from her car at the memorial, was met by the Master Gunner, which honoured title is held now by Field-Marshal the Viscount Alanbrooke. The tall young soldiers of the guard of honour towered over her in their khaki battle-dress as she went along their ranks to make her inspection, studying each

telling how houses were being provided for the regiment's disabled and for the war widows of its dead. They would form another memorial. Then, slipping her hand into her blue purse to bring out a type-written manuscript, she herself addressed this great gathering that stood around the stone howitzer.

Thousands of people looked on. White-aproned nurses filled the windows of St. George's Hospital, just across the roadway. The five hundred troops on parade were outnumbered many times by the Regiment's

Photo : Keystone

Princess Elizabeth at the Royal Artillery Memorial.

man as she passed. A neat feminine figure amid all this military array, she bore herself with great assurance and dignity as befitted the King's daughter.

She had come to Hyde Park Corner on this Sunday morning to unveil additions to the Artillery memorial ; new panels in remembrance of those Gunners who lost their lives in the war that ended only a few summers ago. Standing on the dais, a centre for all eyes, she listened to speeches

old comrades, among whom were winners of that highest of all decorations for bravery, the Victoria Cross. There were six blind men and there were many relatives of the fallen. The V.C.s were given a place of honour near the dais and the blind men sat next to them, seeing nothing of all this.

" This shrine now commemorates for ever the sacrifice of those many thousands of Royal Artillerymen who fought for their King and the freedom of their country in two great wars. . . ." It was a kindly voice, yet firm, unquavering and full of character that the blind men heard speaking now. " The King, Colonel-in-Chief of the Royal Regiment of Artillery, has asked me to convey to you his pride in the Regiment and his sympathy with all the relatives of the fallen. . . ."

The new memorial was unveiled and dedicated. The drums rolled three times, then died away and the sad, lingering trumpet notes of " Last Post " rose upon the stillness. When they, too, faded, the quietness deepened into silence and for two minutes no man moved or made a sound. Again the drums rolled, then there sounded the Royal-Artillery regimental call. High up on the roof of the great hospital, where the trumpeters stood silhouetted against the sky, the trumpets answered—" Reveille."

Khaki trousers and heavy Army boots showed below the cassocks of the military choir leading the singing of the hymn that followed. The collars of their battledress tunics were edged above their white surplices.

When wreaths had been laid and the Benediction pronounced, the young lady in blue drove slowly away down Constitution Hill to return to Buckingham Palace.

Three hours later people standing outside the Palace gates saw her drive out again, noting now that she was dressed in green; lime green. This time, the car drove across to Birdcage Walk and into Wellington Barracks, little more than a stone-throw away.

The men who mustered in their civilian clothes on the parade ground here had all seen service in that famous Regiment, the Grenadier Guards. Reunited briefly now through their Comrades' Association, they gathered about the King's daughter, the Colonel of their Regiment, at this brief drumhead service. Drums piled upon one another in front of the bomb-wrecked chapel formed an altar, as they have done on many a field of battle. This was the prayer that the clergy murmured :

" *Almighty Father, vouchsafe, we beseech Thee, to bless the Grenadier Regiment of Foot Guards, its Colonel, Her Royal Highness the Princess Elizabeth, Duchess of Edinburgh, and all its members, both past and present. Help them to live their lives in true loyalty to Thee, to our King and to each other ; so that, bound together in the brotherhood of the Regiment, they may show forth the true meaning of comradeship wherever they may be. . . . Amen.*"

The ex-Grenadier comrades marched away towards Whitehall to place a wreath upon the Guards Memorial which stands facing Horse Guards Parade. Then they came swinging back up the Mall, led by a Grenadiers' band in scarlet and tall bearskins. Not all the assortment of civilian clothes could hide the fact that they were Guardsmen. They marched proudly, as they were entitled with all that tradition of valour behind them, and their heads were held high as they went past the Palace to the tune of *The British Grenadier.*

Their Colonel, the young lady in green, took their salutes as she stood upon a dais in front of her father's house.

ROYAL OCCASIONS IN JUNE

THURSDAY, JUNE 2, 1949. Up in Edinburgh, the Duke of Gloucester, who this year was appointed by the King to be Lord High Commissioner to the General Assembly of the Church of Scotland, yesterday saw the deliberations of that venerable court come to an end after a week of debate. It is nearly four hundred years since the first Assembly met and, since then, there have been many Lord High Commissioners. But none of them, thought the Duke, could have been more impressed than he had been by the high standard of debates, the atmosphere of sincerity and conviction and by the thrust and parry of argument. " You have taught me much, for which I will ever be grateful," he said. " I have a deeper insight than ever I had before into the life and work of the Church, with its width and splendour of vision, its dynamic vigour and its selfless and devoted service to mankind."

If the Duke was impressed by this General Assembly, it is also true to say, from all accounts, that his own address on the opening day made a deep impression on all who heard it.

This was one of the most important among the Duke's many and varied engagements this year. He and the Duchess were in residence at the Palace of Holyroodhouse.

Photo: The Scotsman

The Duke of Gloucester, as Lord High Commissioner to the General Assembly of the Church of Scotland, walking in procession with the Duchess to St. Giles' Cathedral, Edinburgh.

Photo: Daily Graphic

June 4 :   Queen Mary, arriving for the Derby at Epsom, is greeted by Lord Rosebery, one of the Stewards of the Meeting.   In the centre is the Earl of Athlone, her brother. Queen Mary watched the race from the Royal box with the Queen, Princess Elizabeth, the Duke of Edinburgh and the Princess Royal.

Photo: Planet News

June 6 :   The Duke of Edinburgh, wearing sun-glasses, chats with F. Wilt (U.S.A.), one of the competitors in the British Games at the White City.   The Duke is patron of the Games.

THURSDAY, JUNE 9, 1949. " His Majesty the King has graciously intimated his intention of being present at the Ceremony of Trooping the Colour on the Horse Guards Parade at 11.00 hours." Thus the special Order of the Brigade of Guards, issued for to-day's celebration of the King's official birthday ; " official " as distinct from the actual date of his birth which was on December 14, in 1895.

All the pageantry of pre-war days was brought back again, painting the scene with scarlet and gold, for this traditional military ceremony. Drab khaki had no place here and battledress might never have been heard of in the British Army for all that was seen of it.

Two ceremonies are embraced in Trooping the Colour. It is an elaborate guard-mounting parade deriving from the old custom of " Lodging the Colours " in a place of safety which would form a rallying point in the event of sudden attack. It is also a birthday review. Claimed by many to be one of the finest military parades in the world, it is at the same time one of London's free spectacles and proof once again, adjudged spectators, that " No one can do these things quite like the Guards."

On this grey and overcast morning, the packed thousands outside the Palace thrilled to the sight of the King driving out of the wide centre gateway and down the leafy Mall ; a soldierly, erect figure in full-dress Guards uniform. He sat alone in an open landau drawn by two greys.

A Sovereign's escort of the Household Cavalry—the Life Guards and the Royal Horse Guards (" The Blues ")—rode in front and behind the carriage, each helmeted trooper on his black charger a member of a Royal bodyguard that was raised by King Charles II in the year 1661. The gleam of their silvered helmets matched the glint of each trooper's cuirass, bright as lightning.

Immediately behind the King's carriage came Princess Elizabeth, mounted side-saddle on a chestnut horse and wearing a habit of dark blue, the colour of the Guards' undress uniform. She wore her badges of rank as Colonel of the Grenadiers. The Garter riband cut its vivid light blue band across her tunic and round her waist was the gold and crimson ceremonial belt of a Guards officer. The Grenadiers badge stood out in gold against the blue of her peaked cap. They must have been very proud to-day, I think, in the Grenadier Regiment of Foot Guards. Side by side with the Princess, rode her uncle, the Duke of Gloucester, who is Colonel of the Scots Guards.

Eleven o'clock struck as the head of the King's procession entered the parade ground. His Majesty stood in his carriage for the Royal Salute, then drove out to inspect the Line and the cavalry escort. While the complicated parade continued, with all its impressive movements and its superb drill, the King remained seated on a dais at the saluting base. The drums beat. The Colour was displayed and carried high along the ranks of rigid Guardsmen. The massed bands marched and counter-marched across the parade ground and the officers led their troops twice past the King, now standing at the saluting base, first in a slow, and then a quick, march. The Queen with Queen Mary and Princess Margaret, the Duchess of Gloucester and the Duchess of Kent, watched from a window above Horse Guards Arch.

Such was the exactness of the timing that at the precise moment that the Royal Salute was given again at the end of the ceremony, the clock on Horse Guards Parade struck twelve and the saluting guns began to fire in Hyde Park.

Now came an impressive moment. The officer in command of the parade rode over to the King's carriage.

" *Your Guards are ready, sir*," he said.

Princess Elizabeth and the Duke of Gloucester ride together at the ceremony of Trooping the Colour.

A general scene of the Trooping
the Colour ceremony.

Photo: P.A.-Reuter

Royal spectators on the balcony of Buckingham Palace watching the King returning after the Trooping the Colour ceremony. On the balcony are (left to right) : the Princess Royal, the Queen, the Princess Marie Louise, the Duchess of Gloucester (speaking to her younger son, Prince Richard), Queen Mary, the Duchess of Kent and Princess Margaret. Standing in front of the Princess Royal is Prince William of Gloucester. Next to Prince Richard is Prince Michael of Kent.

Photo: Keystone

" *Once again the King took the salute, standing this time on a dais outside the Palace as his Guards went by. His daughter and his brother now rode at their head.*" Princess Elizabeth and the Duke of Gloucester salute the King.

The King nodded assent.

" *To your duties ! Quick march !* " The commanding officer's order rang out, clear and strong, across the parade ground.

And so, with the King at their head and the Princess and the Duke riding behind him, the Guardsmen marched to Buckingham Palace. The King led them up the Mall and they marched to the tune of " The Red Cloak " and " Sons of the Brave " and " The Mad Major ". There has been no braver sight in London for a long time. The crowd's cheers swept the Mall.

Once again the King took the salute, standing this time on a dais outside the Palace as his Guards went by. His daughter and his brother now rode at their head. In the palace forecourt, the old guard and the new guard, about to take over their duties, were drawn up facing one another. The King, one hand on his sword hilt and the other raised in salute, paced slowly between them. He walked alone, his equerries following. " God Save the King " played the bands and the Guardsmen presented arms. Slowly the King passed out of sight through the archway. On the balcony, the Queen, the central figure amid the group there, stood with hands clasped in front of her looking down at him.

FRIDAY, JUNE 17, 1949. The rhododendrons inform the traveller from Virginia Water that he is nearing Ascot. They peep over the fences that run beside the road and ramble in profusion through the woodlands where all the silver birch alone would be beauty enough without this additional glory. Then, when our traveller comes to Ascot's long wide street and finds it full of fashion with women's silks and men's grey toppers, he will know that there is racing on the heath and that this is the Royal meeting. As additional evidence, he may note that there are strawberries for sale outside the licensed premises of the Horse and Groom. Back

in London, the clubs in St. James's and Pall Mall will be strangely empty.

Epsom on Derby Day is a gigantic holiday. Ascot has more of the garden party atmosphere about it. This year, however, the fashion experts declared themselves, in general, to be greatly disappointed in the dresses chosen to grace the first coupon-free meeting since the war. The men have a great advantage here. They can produce the same top hat and morning coat from year to year without much comment from anybody, excepting, perhaps, the critical *Tailor and Cutter* which has these matters very much at heart. All this, be it said, has no influence one way or the other on the excellence of the racing.

Cream and pale green is the colour scheme of the Ascot stands. It is repeated again in the long row of innumerable private boxes that run in tiers for some two hundred yards behind all the bookmakers laying the odds so energetically in their enclosure. The white-railed paddock is a pleasant spot, gently shaded by its trees under one of which there was to be seen on each day of the meeting a horse box which came (so said the notice on the side) from a home of rest for horses. It was there as a precaution in the event of accident, not as an invitation to tired non-stayers. The area around the totalisator is littered at the end of each day with discarded betting slips of the more unfortunate backers but each morning is as spick and span again as the Royal Enclosure itself. At the far end of the paddock are the Club tents ; not as numerous or as spacious or as well-provisioned as in more leisurely and ample days but none the less maintaining the traditions of hospitality set for them in years gone by.

Eagle-eyed attendants guard the entrances to the Royal Enclosure as keenly as an army recruit going about his first sentry duty. A small oblong cardboard badge, with a crown in one corner and the name of the holder clearly inscribed in ink, is the passport here. It is strictly not transferable, must be worn so as to be distinctly seen by the officials. No money is refunded for lost or mislaid badges but considerable safeguard is made against this by the attachment of a most substantial steel fastening pin. Needless to say, there are no bookmakers here, though backers may confide their wishes (no money passing) to the various firms whose representatives lean so confidentially over the railings at one side of the lawn.

The Royal Box, decorated again this year with blue hydrangeas, overlooks the front lawn of the Enclosure. This position gives its occupants an excellent view of the finish and enables the crowds on the heath opposite to get an equally good view of the royal racegoers.

We have to thank Queen Anne for Ascot, for it was she who ordered a course to be laid out there and made it known by means of the *London Gazette*, that : " Her Majesty's plate of 100 guineas will be run for round the new heat on Ascot Common. near Windsor . . . by any horse, mare or gelding, being no more than six years old the grass before, as must be certified under the hand of the breeder, carrying 12st., three heats, to be entered the last day of July at Mr. Hancock's, at Fern Hill, near the starting post." The day was an August Saturday in the year 1711 when Queen Anne and her suite drove over from Windsor Castle for the opening of the new course. It must have been a beautiful spot in those days and the years since have treated it with kindness. The heath—embracing now a golf course—and the woodlands beyond have a green and pleasant sweep that make Ascot well-remembered by all its visitors.

On each of the four days racing this week, ending in mellow sunshine this afternoon, the King and Queen have made the drive from Windsor Castle, where they have been in residence. Nowadays, the journey is achieved partly by motor-car— which Queen Anne did not foresee, it may very safely be assumed—and continues from a point known as Duke's Lane by means of a horse-drawn carriage procession, with all the elegance that that implies. It is a picturesque and memorable sight as the carriages come up the finishing straight, past the packed stands, and the tiers of boxes and the lawn of the Royal Enclosure on the left ; cheered by the crowds opposite, pressing against the rails on the heath side, which is as free for all as it was in 1711.

No one in the royal party followed the racing more keenly than Princess Elizabeth. She and Princess Margaret were there each day, driving in the second carriage of the procession with the Duke of Edinburgh. They both wore different dresses on each of the four days and I, for one, would not like to say on which of them they looked the most charming. They stayed until the last minute of every day's racing, though the King and Queen left earlier ; they made frequent visits to the paddock and quite obviously thoroughly enjoyed themselves.

The weather chopped and changed a good deal between sunshine and dullness but no rain fell during the meeting. There was some excellent racing in which the victory of Lord Derby's Alycidon over the American-bred Black Tarquin in the Gold Cup on Thursday was one of the highlights. It was good to see an English horse carry off this great race after three years of foreign successes. And on Wednesday, the second day of the meeting, when the King took the Coronation Stakes with Avila, there could have been no more popular win.

MONDAY, JUNE 20, 1949. Once again the Royal Tournament has opened its doors at vast Olympia and, afternoon and evening, is now staging its displays there. It is a never-failing attraction in the London scene at this time of the year, making its appeal

The King and Queen driving up the course on the opening day of Royal Ascot.

alike to young and old. They turn up in their thousands to see it and the charities of the Services benefit accordingly. This afternoon, Princess Elizabeth, the Duke of Edinburgh and Princess Margaret gave the tournament the encouragement of their attendance.

The old favourites take their customary pride of place in the daily programmes. Those keen rivals, Chatham and Devonport —each team cheered by its supporters in the most unblushing way—fight it out against the stop-watches of the timekeepers as they sling their naval field guns across five-feet high walls and a supposedly bottom-less chasm. Portsmouth and Naval Air Command, the other competing teams, were to-day taking an afternoon's rest from all this toil ; they go into action again to-night. This event, which arouses among the partisans nearly as much excitement as a Chelsea goal against Arsenal, is always most fiercely contested. The pace is terrific. " Lift quick, run fast, eyes in the boat—and no penalties " is the slogan of the crews.

Devonport beat Chatham this afternoon with the very good time of 3 minutes 55 seconds (the record to date, set up by Devonport Stokers in 1938 is 3 mins. 48 secs.) " All the Nice Girls Love a Sailor," played the band as both teams marched out, still jaunty despite their exertions.

Another favourite, of course, is the musical ride of the Household Cavalry. It is all the more effective at Olympia because, indoors, one can hear all that pleasant jingling of the harness. The King's Troop of the Royal Horse Artillery, galloping with their gun carriages at an average speed of about twenty miles an hour, brought dash and colour to the arena. It is this unit, stationed at St. John's Wood barracks, which fires the ceremonial salutes in Hyde Park. Awakening recollections of pre-mechanization days, the Troop's drive stands in vivid contrast to the show put on by those acrobats of the motor cycle, the despatch riders of the Royal Signals, who, on this occasion, do very nearly everything except carry despatches. The great nerve

Photo: Daily Graphic

Princess Elizabeth, the Duke of Edinburgh and Princess Margaret in the royal box at the Royal Tournament at Olympia.

and skill they show is all the more remarkable when one remembers that most of the members of to-day's team were recruits.

The "Sappers"—linked, so the programme said, with the King's Engineers or Ingeniators who were in being in 1066—showed how to build a 40-feet bridge in the remarkable time of 8 minutes 21 seconds. That would undoubtedly have surprised the Ingeniators. The R.A.F. came out this year with a display by their Alsatian police dogs which are proving of enormous value, particularly on lonely airfields where, at night, one dog is reckoned to be worth a dozen men. Each dog works with a Service policeman whose commands he is trained to obey. The exhibition provided very good proof of how well the dogs would be able to deal with any intruder. We had,

too, parachute drops from up near the roof. At 105 feet, of course, the parachutes had to be already open before the drop was made. A woman nursing orderly and a nursing sister showed that they could do it as well as the men. The R.A.F. trains all British parachute troops. Since 1941, over half a million descents have been made at No. 1 Parachute Training School which is now at Upper Heyford, in Oxfordshire. The accident rate works out at one minor injury in every 1,000 descents.

The immaculate Marines marched and drilled, the Guards' massed drums and pipes made martial music, the super-fit gymnasts of the three fighting Services vaulted their high horses with incredible ease. There was never a dull moment nor, so swiftly did one event follow the other, an empty arena.

Photo: The Times

June 21 : Princess Margaret declaring open new premises of the English Speaking Union in Charles Street, London. Among those on the platform are Lord Salisbury, the President, and Mr. Lewis Douglas, the American Ambassador.

The start of the Channel Islands tour. The Princess and the Duke go aboard H.M.S.
Anson and are received by the captain of the ship.

FRIDAY, JUNE 24, 1949. At ten minutes to six on Tuesday evening, the training battleship *Anson*, which had sailed from Portland that afternoon for the Channel Islands, dropped anchor in waters off Alderney. The escorting destroyers *Wizard* and *Roebuck* anchored nearby.

From the deck of the battleship, Princess Elizabeth and the Duke of Edinburgh examined through their glasses the fortifications which the Germans had built with slave labour during their occupation of the island. The cliffs bristled with them. Then, going ashore, they heard at first-hand this small island's wartime story. At the approach of the Germans, the islanders were ordered to evacuate Alderney in June 1940. " We were all like one big family on our island," said an old man. " All our days were happy days before the war came. It broke our hearts to go, leaving our homes and belongings. The years seemed so long before we could come back. And when we did return, we cried to look at what they had done to our island." There was sadness in his voice even now. Then he smiled, remembering the happy days. " It will come back again," he said. " It will take time but we shall get the island right again."

The visit of the Princess and her husband warmed the hearts of the islanders to their

Photo: Daily Graphic

A happy Alderney incident.

A Jersey crowd scene.

Photo: Daily Graphic

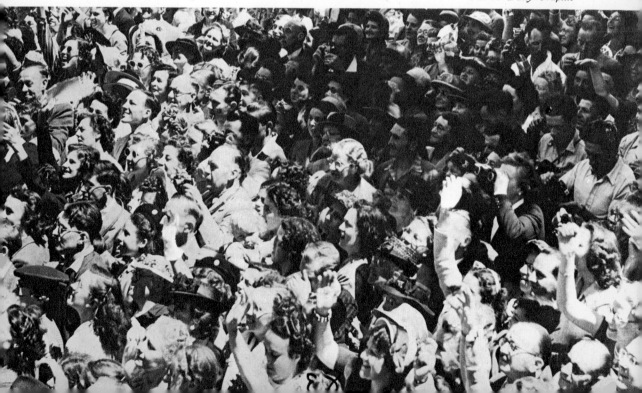

work of recovery. They gathered on the small plateau above the harbour town of St. Anne. Here, on the public assembly ground, Alderney's official reception was staged with simplicity in the evening sunshine. The men of the British Legion paraded with their banners. The young schoolgirls came dressed in their summer frocks to wave their Union Jacks as enthusiastically as the boys. Very nearly half the population must have been there ; the other half was waiting in the town square. Everyone gathered round to hear the Princess. " A small but very precious jewel in the Crown," was how she described Alderney, and for the moment, as she spoke all the war-time ravages of the occupation were forgotten.

Wild flowers from the Alderney fields decorated the spokes of some of the assortment of cars that drove in procession through the narrow streets of the town. In the square the Princess planted a tree to commemorate a visit that, one felt, had done inestimable good. Watching from the high land when it was all over, the people of Alderney could see the fast barge flying the Princess's standard speed out across the bay back to the battleship. In *Anson* that night, the Princess and the Duke dined informally with the ship's officers in the wardroom where, after dinner, one of those cheerful naval parties got under way. The Duke joined in the singing of the sea chanties with gusto.

Jersey was the next of the islands to be visited and all of Wednesday was spent there. Thousands of holidaymakers, enjoying Jersey's blue skies and warm sunshine, joined in the welcome at St. Helier. On such a day as this, the German occupation must have seemed a nightmare, best forgotten ; the Princess recalled it only to offer her praise to the men and women of the island. The spirit of the Channel Islanders was unbroken and they lost neither faith nor hope, she said. Jersey's people were faithful subjects of the Dukes of Normandy, even before they ascended the Throne of England, recalled the Princess.

The yachtsmen of St. Helier are rightly proud of a wartime exploit when they helped to assist in the evacuation of British troops from St. Malo in June 1940. Eighteen yachts put out in two convoys to the rescue. The first small group of four ferried troops and stores out to the improvised transports, many of which were potato boats from Jersey lying off-shore. Meanwhile, the remaining yachts, several of which had been laid up, were being fitted out ready for the job. They followed twenty-four hours later. All of them remained at St. Malo until the demolition party ashore had done its work in the docks, then they went in and brought the last of the troops off. There was not much time to spare. Advance elements of a German mobile column entered the port area as the yachts were leaving the outer roads.

" Well done," signalled the Admiralty to the Commodore of the Club, a message that had to be kept hidden throughout the German occupation. The Duke, having heard of all this, went down to meet these brave yachtsmen and gave them his hand.

Sark, smaller even than Alderney, was the third of the islands to be visited. Here is a dreamy, peaceful place where time has stood still and life moves happily, serenely on from day to day. There was nothing very tranquil, however, about the motor torpedo boat in which the Princess and the Duke crossed at a speed of twenty-five knots from *Anson*, anchored in Guernsey roads. The thrill of this, with the boat literally leaping out of the water and churning up its spectacular wake, made the contrast all the greater when they went ashore—not without some difficulty for the Princess who had to make a jump for it—at miniature La Maseline harbour. This must surely be one of the smallest harbours in the world.

Something of the atmosphere of this place may be gathered from the terms of the loyal address read by the Seigneur who with La Dame, his wife, received the visitors on the quayside. In part, it ran :

"*In this island, granted in 1565 by Her Gracious Majesty the Queen Elizabeth of happy memory to Helier de Carteret, Lord of the Seigneurie of Saint Ouen in the Island of Jersey, the laws and customs then prevailing have continued substantially unaltered to the present time, and we would not have it otherwise, for we believe that they serve our purpose and meet our needs.*

"*We yield to none in our loyalty to the Crown and in our affection for the members of your Royal House, and we humbly pray that the blessing of Almighty God may always rest upon Your Royal Highnesses and upon your son, the Prince Charles.*"

There are no motor-cars on Sark ; a factor which adds a great deal to its peace and, probably, a little to the longevity of some of its inhabitants. In recent years, however, the ubiquitous farm tractor has crept in, giving rise to no inconsiderable controversy whether it should, or should not, be allowed on the roads. The population of the island—"which means those who live here in the winter," was how my informant described it—is in the region of a mere five hundred.

The Salvation Army Band, imported for the occasion from Guernsey, played the National Anthem on the quayside, the Duke made a short speech declaring the new harbour open and so began one of the most charming and delightful Royal visits it has fallen to my lot to record.

Sitting side by side in an old-fashioned carriage drawn by a plodding white horse, the Princess and the Duke drove up the

Photo: Photographic News

On peaceful Sark. "*Up the steep, dusty road leading inland from the sea.*"

steep, dusty road leading inland from the sea. The islanders threw in little bunches of flowers as the carriage passed by. The church bells were ringing across the meadows. There was honeysuckle in the hedges and an archway of flowers stretching across the country road. Neither the white horse, plodding steadily along, nor the driver, Charlie Perree, in his best blue suit and new cloth cap, seemed in any hurry.

Two other carriages followed, making up the small procession. The equerry was perched on the box seat of the second one in which travelled the Princess's Lady-in-Waiting and the Comptroller of her Household. La Dame, the Seigneur and the Home Secretary, Mr. Chuter Ede, who had come from London to be in attendance at each of the islands, occupied the third. Everybody else walked. It was most enjoyable strolling along in the sunshine.

" I think we'll trot now," ordered the Seigneur as the gentle procession approached the Seigneurie. One of the Sark girls walking alongside was sent forward to tell Charlie Perree. The white horse jogged forward a little faster. But the travellers on foot walked leisurely on behind ; all, that is, except the photographers. They trotted, too.

From the quiet of Sark, the M.T.B. dashed across to Guernsey where the Bailiff welcomed the Princess as " a sailor's daughter and a sailor's wife." The afternoon and evening were spent amid the island people here and in her speech the Princess said she saw with admiration the work which had been done to blot out the ugly relics of war and to restore to Guernsey the peace, prosperity and happiness which were her right and her tradition through the centuries.

At 2.30 a.m. to-day, *Anson* sailed for the mainland and at the more congenial hour of 9.25, the Princess and the Duke embarked with considerable naval ceremony in the destroyer *Wizard* which, an hour later,

sailed gently into Dartmouth Harbour. It was while he was a cadet at the Royal Naval College at Dartmouth that the Duke had one of his earliest meetings with the Princess when she was accompanying the King and Queen. Now he returned with her to receive the salutes of the present-day cadets, to make a tour of inspection of the college and to renew old acquaintances among the staff.

Looking over the shoulder of a fair-haired young lad in the laboratory, the Duke found him struggling with the problem : " To determine Joule's electrical equivalent of heat energy." He smiled reflectively, perhaps remembering when he as a lad was confronted with the same task.

SATURDAY, JUNE 25, 1949. The Duchess of Kent who, week in and week out, fulfils the fullest possible round of public engagements, returned to London yesterday from a visit to Wales. During her tour there, she went down the Bargoed Steam Coal Colliery mine. Over her fashionable strawberry two-piece suit with its gay white polka dots, the Duchess slipped on a brown mackintosh. She exchanged her white hat for a brown turban and a miner's helmet. Then she went underground, right to the coal face, where she watched work going on and asked to see a demonstration of the water infusion system employed to allay the dust.

The Duchess's life is one of wide interests. Her public duties and the upbringing of her young family of three occupy much of her time. There is Prince Edward, the young Duke of Kent, now nearly fourteen years old, who seems each year to grow in appearance more and more like his father, killed in that sad flying accident during the war. Prince Edward is now at Eton where, in the tradition of that famous school, he is accorded no special indulgence because of his high station—and none is sought on his behalf. Between the hours of study, he may

A Guernsey garden party in the sunshine. Princess Elizabeth is seated at the centre table.

frequently be seen on the river or out on the playing fields ; a pleasant-looking, fair-haired young boy with rather a shy smile and an engaging manner. Like so many other boys nowadays, the Duke, one gathers, is intensely mechanically-minded.

Princess Alexandra, who is fourteen months younger, is at an English girls' school. She has her mother's features. Prince Michael, the youngest, has a governess to look after him at " Coppins ", the Duchess's charming house at Iver, some twenty miles out of London, in Buckinghamshire.

Many good causes have the Duchess's patronage and helpful support. There is, to instance but one, the R.A.F. Benevolent Fund, of which she is President, an office in which she succeeded her husband when he was killed on active service during the war. Like the late Duke, the Duchess takes a great personal interest in many of the cases that come within the province of the fund.

She has known great sorrow herself and those who meet her—at a hospital, perhaps, or a home for old people—often comment on her qualities of sympathy and kindly understanding.

The Duchess's private interests, outside the family life, are largely centred in the arts.

WEDNESDAY, JUNE 29, 1949. Their Channel Islands tour over, the Princess and the Duke were soon off again, this time to Cheshire, to the hills and dales of Derbyshire and to Nottingham, celebrating the granting of its Charter by Henry the Sixth five hundred years ago, where Robin Hood, complete with bow and arrow, was postered everywhere.

They left London on Sunday night, slept in the train, arrived at Macclesfield (waiting to show its good wishes and its silks) at ten o'clock the following morning, then carried on through the day until 8 p.m., at which hour respite and rest was sought in a return to the train.

There is nothing leisurely about a Royal tour like this. The first day's programme —ten hours long on one of the hottest days of the year—might well be regarded as a feat of physical endurance. Yet at the end of it all, having smiled her way through miles and miles of crowded streets, shaken hands countless times, replied to a civic address of welcome, inspected a silk mill and a china works, formally opened the main door of Derby's new Council House and appeared on the balcony, listened to a second mayoral address and attended a war memorial service, the Princess looked just as charming in her silk taffeta frock as when she first stepped from the train. The Duke took it all gaily in his stride. Not everybody, by a very long way, could do it.

At Macclesfield, where the staple industry has long been the production of silk, to which must now be added nylon and rayon, the Princess and the Duke toured one of the mills at length. It was in 1745 that this firm was founded in Macclesfield. But long before that, the family who owned it, the Brockle-hursts, were making silk and mohair-covered buttons in their homes. Some of the buttons found their way to customers in places as far away as Amsterdam and Moscow.

Presents of silk for his parents were accompanied by a gift of some silk handker-chiefs for Prince Charles. The firm's elegant brochure recalled Prince Charlie and his Highlanders marching victoriously into the town over two hundred years ago.

From Macclesfield, the route lay by way of a high Peak District road, along which a group of cheery souls waited outside the Cat and Fiddle public house to pay their respects ; then it dropped down to Buxton, where the fifteen-years-old Queen of the well-dressing festival made her pretty curtsey at St. Ann's Well and the Mayor offered the town's loyal greetings. Derby was reached in the afternoon and here the Princess and the Duke stayed until nearly eight o'clcock in the evening.

While the Princess went off to see the Crown Derby china works, the Duke was touring the Rolls-Royce works and meeting workers there. They joined up again at the latter place where they stood together before the Battle of Britain memorial window. Dominating this, the figure of a typical fighter pilot of the R.A.F. stands on the spinner of an airscrew. He is ready for the Battle, in flying boots and " Mae West ", his helmet in his hands. Later, at the Council House, the great crowd staged a tremendous reception scene when the Princess and her husband came out together on to the balcony. Everywhere they go, up and down the country, there is a very sincere welcome for them.

The day's final ceremony, the laying of the foundation stone of a model village for the disabled, which Derby is building as a war memorial, produced another impressive speech by the Princess. The plan is to have about sixty houses and bungalows, a community centre, a bowling green and a children's playground. In the village will live disabled members and former members of the Services, people disabled while at work and their relatives and dependants.

" It is at once a memorial to the fallen and an enterprise for the living," declared the Princess. " I am sure that those whom this war memorial honours would have been the first to approve its purpose. A memorial should indeed remind all who look upon it of the value

Photo: Nottingham Guardian

At Nottingham, crowds on the Victoria Embankment break the cordon and close in on the royal car.

and self-sacrifice it commemorates. But, just as the men who died performed the greatest service for their fellow countrymen, so the memorial we raise to them should serve those that follow after. In years to come, when my husband and I revisit this town, we shall look forward to finding at this place a flourishing community where the fallen are not forgotten but where the debt which we owe them is paid in service to the new generation. When, as this evening, we stand united in the recollection of those who gave all they had for us, and pray God to make us worthy of their example, our own quarrels, our complaints and our daily worries shrink into insignificance and we are left with a truer sense of values. The greatest tribute we can pay to the fallen is, by remembering them, to improve ourselves.

Photo: Daily Graphic

" Nearly five hundred schoolgirls in bright-coloured dresses whirled their gay and happy country dances in the square in front of. the Council House." A Nottingham interlude.

Therefore, it is not enough to praise their courage and unselfishness. Each of us in our own lives and in our own way can raise a memorial still greater than anything built of brick or stone."

Sharp at ten o'clock the next morning, when the special train on which the Princess and the Duke had spent the night pulled into the Midland Station, the Nottingham programme started. The city exhibited the products of its present-day industries (there are over 135 of them with 2,731 factories) at the Trades Exhibition with as much pride as, later, it displayed its ancient charters, the earliest of which bore the date 1155.

Unflaggingly, the Exhibition was inspected as to its lace, its bicycles, its cricket bats, even its aspirins, one of which the Duke pocketed with naval resourcefulness against the day's emergencies. He also ordered from that notable firm of cricket bat makers, Messrs. Gunn and Moore, a small implement for the future use of little Prince Charles who is obviously destined to be introduced to our national game at a very early age.

There was a delightful interlude after the official luncheon when nearly five hundred schoolgirls in bright-coloured dresses whirled their gay and happy country dances in the square in front of the Council House. Then on to the Forest ; an arena this afternoon for school sports. Here, the Duke met his war-time naval batman, now a trolley-bus driver, and his wife ; he enquired most earnestly how his former servant was prospering ; and how went the trolley-bus driving ? " I hope you're looking after him," he said to the wife.

Everywhere along the twenty miles of streets toured during the morning and afternoon, the crowds were so thick that the Mayor said afterwards : " I thought Nottingham had a population of 300,000 but it looked to me more like 3,000,000 to-day." The Princess and the Duke must have felt a little tired by the time five o'clock came. But they showed no sign of it.

Mansfield had a brief glimpse of them to-day when they stopped in the town on their way to the green and pleasant area of

Photo : Nottingham Guardian

The Duke meets his war-time naval batman, now a trolley-bus driver.

Harlow Wood. Here the Princess laid another foundation stone, this time of the Portland Training College where disabled people from four counties—Nottingham, Derby, Lincoln and Leicester—will receive special training to fit them for such work as their courage, overcoming their disabilities, will enable them to undertake.

Photo: Daily Graphic

June 29 : Princess Margaret arriving at the Victoria League Ball at the Dorchester Hotel, London. With her is Princess Alice, Countess of Athlone, who is President of the League.

THURSDAY, JUNE 30, 1949. This afternoon, at Woodford Green in Essex, there was to be seen the unusual sight of the President of the M.C.C., the Duke of Edinburgh, dressed in a dark blue lounge suit and a stiff white collar, thoroughly enjoying himself as he cracked the bowling of some middle-aged gentlemen about in a net set up in the pleasant grounds of the White House. The Essex County Playing Fields Association was holding a luncheon and a garden party there. The object of the luncheon was to gain for the movement the support of prominent Essex business men, each one of whom found himself confronted with an excellent plate of cold chicken and a donation form.

The Duke has been throwing all his energy and enthusiasm into the playing fields movement since he took over the Presidency of the National Association. He is, it is plain to see, a young man who likes to get results, as witness his remark the other day when given a birthday party by some of those connected with the organization. "I don't care how many birthday parties you give me," he said; "I still want those playing fields!" He himself has been addressing meetings in various parts of the country to gain support but, as a member of the Royal Family, makes no direct appeal for funds himself. That is left to others who follow when the Duke has laid the bait.

At luncheon to-day, he set out the working plan of the Association with commendable clarity and brevity. "We believe everyone must have somewhere to play organized games and unorganized games," he said. "We know that at the moment there are not enough playing fields. Therefore, our sole aim—and in good military circles you only have one aim—is to provide the necessary playing fields." There was a typical touch of humour in the remark that the Association had accumulated twenty-five years experience—"which, if you work it out, you can't accumulate in any shorter time."

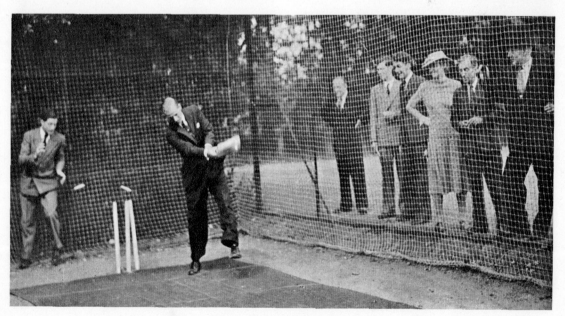

Photo: Photographic News

Clean bowled, leg stump! The Duke of Edinburgh has a knock in the nets at Woodford Green.

Then came the little bit of cricket. It was very sporting of the Duke to join in. He and his equerry put down a few balls—he bowls a useful, medium-pace off-spinner—and then the Duke had a knock himself. Much to the delight of the photographers, he was bowled neck and crop first ball but afterwards proceeded to tackle the bowling in the most workmanlike way. There were no more Royal wickets for the aspiring trundlers.

" What about a cup of tea ? " suggested the perspiring President of the M.C.C., as he left the net.

Photo: P.A.-Reuter

July 1 :   The Duchess of Kent presents the cup to Ted Schroeder, American winner of the men's singles at Wimbledon.

A JULY JOURNAL

FRIDAY, JULY 1, 1949. To-day, when that great and glorious country celebrated its eighty-second birthday, Canada's flag flew over Westminster Abbey. And, at noon, the King and Queen, driving from Buckingham Palace, joined Canadians in London at their Dominion Day service there.

The voice of Canada sounded young and strong and clear within the Abbey walls.

O Canada ! Our Home and Native Land !
True patriot love in all thy sons command.
With glowing hearts we see thee rise,
The True North, strong and free,
And stand on guard, O Canada,
We stand on guard for thee.

So sang the choir and congregation, conjuring up pictures and memories of prairie, forest and mountain, of vast lakes and wide rivers ; of busy cities with famous names and unknown, isolated townships in the backwoods.

The Lesson was read by the Canadian High Commissioner in London and the address was delivered by another Canadian, Dr. John Lowe, who is Dean of Christ Church and Vice-Chancellor of Oxford University. " Perhaps, most of all, we are proud and happy that while every freedom has been preserved and every proper national aspiration satisfied, the links which connect us with the other members of this family of nations have never been broken," said Dr. Lowe. He spoke of the King as the common head of that family. " We

sons of Canada on this Dominion Day pay our humble and affectionate tribute to him," he said. " We also wish to be allowed to salute his gracious partner in majesty and in service. We have learned through them that true royalty is not diminished but enhanced by unremitting service on behalf of all their peoples."

Two royal chairs and faldstools, made of Canadian birch, were entrusted by the Honorary Secretary of the Canada Club to the keeping of the Dean and Chapter, being given in memory of those many Canadians who died on active service.

MONDAY, JULY 4, 1949. At two o'clock precisely this afternoon, Princess Elizabeth's standard was to be seen flying for the first time from the roof of Clarence House, in St. James's. It was the outward and visible sign that she and the Duke have now taken up residence there. From Buckingham Palace, not many hundred yards away, the standard could be seen above the treetops. A few minutes after it appeared, sentries of the Welsh Guards, in their scarlet, were posted outside the gateway of the house and, with bayonets fixed, now stand guard.

The Princess and the Duke have had to wait a long time, almost two years, for this London house. It was shortly before their marriage that it was announced that Clarence House was to be their official residence. But the work of repair and

95

Photo: Daily Graphic

The King at the Canadian Dominion Day Service at Westminster Abbey.   With him
is the Dean, Dr. Don.

re-decoration, for which Parliament voted a sum of £50,000, took a good deal longer than was expected. There was much to be done by way of modernizing and the house had not only suffered during the war but had not been lived in for some years.

In the meantime, the Princess and the Duke have had apartments at Buckingham Palace for their use when they were in London. Now, at last, they have a town residence of their own. Queen Mary, at Marlborough House, and the Duke and Duchess of

Gloucester, at York House, are their neighbours. It will, one knows, be a very happy
house.

The mansion, which faces the Mall in
a pleasantly sunny position, was originally
built in 1825 for the Duke of Clarence,
who afterwards became King William IV.
As a modern note, one may remark the
television aerial on the roof. Many of their
wedding presents which have been stored
away until now have been used by the
Princess and the Duke in the furnishing.

There was a domestic interlude of another
kind to-day which caused a great deal of
amusement. It is the yearly habit of some
of the birds that are to be found on the
lake in St. James's Park to fly across to seek
sanctuary and additional quietness within
the Palace gardens, where also there is a
lake, when they are hatching their young.
This safely accomplished, under royal pro-
tection, as it were, the family sets off to
return, on foot, to home waters. The
journey makes an engaging scene, as may
well be imagined.

It was no surprise, quite obviously, to
the sergeant of police on duty at the Palace
gateway when, looking back across the
forecourt, he espied Madame Duck with
four ducklings in line astern coming out of
the garden entrance. He knew his duty
here as surely as if this had been a royal
procession setting out. Madame Duck
came steadily on, making for the railings ;
hesitated a moment before deciding in
favour of some exit nearer the park and
then waddled along to the gateway at the
far end. The sergeant acted as escort,
keeping slow and heavy pace.

Madame panicked a little — and who
is there who will blame her ?—when, at
first, she came face to face with all that
crowd outside the gates. But no charge
of cowardice could be laid against her.
She did not turn back ; she merely hesitated
a moment, as might a young soldier going
over the top. Her offspring waited, com-

plete in faith and blissful in unconcern,
unimpressed one way or the other at this
new aspect of life now opening up before
them. Then brave Madame plucked up
courage and went on ; the call of St. James's
Park must have been very strong. Out of
the great gateway that has often seen the
comings and goings of Kings and Queens,
she went ; and who, again, will be found
to blame her if, momentarily, she waddled
a little faster now, so that for a yard or
so her little brood was hard put to it to keep
pace. They followed as unhesitatingly as
if they were being led on to the safety of a
farm pond, not out into the hurly-burly of
the roadway. All traffic was stopped for
this surprising procession. The car drivers
and the taximen, expecting Royalty, blinked
a little when they saw this strange spectacle.
An American doing the sights of London
enquired with charming naïveté, " Are
these the King's *personal* ducks ? "

Protected and ushered all the way by
the sergeant representative of the law's
strong arm, Madame and her brood completed the Great Adventure safely.

TUESDAY, JULY 5, 1949. Long after
Princess Margaret had left, they were still
talking about her in Islington whose poorer
streets do not often see so much daintiness
and charm, let alone a Royal Princess.

Gaskin Street, where she opened the new
block of flats, could talk of nothing else.
" You should have seen 'er . . . she looked
so lovely," said the middle-aged London
woman who was telling her two friends
about it. " I got home from doing me
shoppin' just in time to see 'er. Came up
past the old Angel, she did. There was
coppers all over the place. Never seen so
many coppers in Gaskin Street in me life."

" What was she wearin' ? " asked the
others. The two of them put the inevitable
feminine question almost in the same breath.
Women always want to know that, whoever

they are, whatever the occasion. I once sat next to a man at a public dinner who obtained a long and detailed description of Princess Elizabeth's dress and jewellery which he proceeded to write down against his wife's questioning. "I daren't go home without it," he confessed. Within ten minutes all the men at his end of the table had copied from him. They would, they confidently anticipated, get full marks for this.

"Let me see now . . . let me see," considered our narrator as to this matter of what Princess Margaret was wearing, before she embarked upon her description. "Well, she had on one of them long, full-skirted silk dresses. Very pretty, it was, with lots of colours in it. And a white hat with a little half-veil. Very smart-looking shoes ; the very latest, ankle-strap and all. They was white. Then she had long white gloves and a white handbag to match.

"She's very slim and slight," the woman went on. "She looked so young beside all the people there, I thought she might be nervous, having to make a speech and all that. She's not nineteen yet, is she ? But it didn't seem to worry her a bit. I couldn't do it, I know that. . . . ."

One of the two friends wanted to know what had happened at the flats.

"Well, first of all the various people got there to receive her," said the woman who was telling the story. "Housing Association people and the Mayor. He was in his red robes. There was a big crowd watching 'em all arrive. Then up drove the Princess. She had a lady with her. That'd be the Lady-in-Waiting, I should think. Then there was a man sitting in the front seat beside the driver. A detective, they said he was. He didn't look like one, though. Out he jumps, opens the door of the car. Then the Princess gets out. Everyone was leaning out of their windows and over the balcony railings. It was a wonder some of 'em didn't fall off.

"Everything was ever so nicely arranged. Pauline Quinn and Betty Sweetman presented the bouquet. They was chosen because they was the first children born on the estate when it started. Then everybody went on to the platform in the yard for the speeches. All the important ones, that is. There was seats in the yard, too, but they was only for people with tickets."

Now the narrator came to the speeches. "First of all, some of the others spoke," she said. "It was all about how bad conditions used to be years ago in some parts of Islington and how the Housing Association was started because of that ; and how they got the first of these flats going. Lady Salisbury was telling all about that. Then Mr. Walters—he's the chairman—he told how this last block of flats they'd built was going to be let to old people. Guess what the rents are ? Thirteen-and-eightpence a week for some and only nine-and-six for the smaller ones. Wonderful, I call it ! Well, then the Mayor he had his say ; and after that the Princess spoke."

The other women wanted to know all about this.

"She's got a nice voice," said their friend and informant. "Very clear and nice to listen to. Not one of them affected voices. I can't stand them. Some of the kids on the balcony started making a bit of a noise when she was talking, but that didn't seem to upset the Princess at all. She just looked up and smiled and went on reading her speech. I can't remember now all she said. But there was one bit that stuck in my mind. She said a lot of people write letters to her about the shortage of houses and she knew how disappointing things could be when you had to keep on waiting.

"Then she went and had a good look at some of the flats and had tea. Everybody started waving when she left and she kept on smiling and waving back. *She really was lovely.*"

A bouquet for Princess Margaret in Gaskin Street, Islington.

THURSDAY, JULY 7, 1949. Strolling on the lawns at a Buckingham Palace garden party, bishops rub shoulders with actors ; politicians beam upon their political enemies and doff their hats most elegantly to one another's wives ; lawyers, Salvationists, admirals, newspaper editors sip their tea standing side-by-side at the 120-yards-long tented refreshment pavilion where the neat Lyons " nippies " serve so expertly and unobtrusively ; Indian women, all dark grace in their bright-coloured silks, move slowly across the garden ; visitors from the Empire countries vie with one another to catch their first glimpse of members of the Royal Family.

Just over six thousand guests had the honour of being invited to the Palace to-day for the first of two such parties which the King and Queen are giving this summer. The weather was grey and chilly, with rain threatening. This set yet another dress problem for the ladies which most of them solved by wearing light coats or furs over their summer frocks. Many brought umbrellas.

Apart from those in uniform, the men were, in the main, in formal morning dress with grey top hats. Lounge suits, however, are not forbidden at Buckingham Palace in these austere days and a sprinkling came so attired. Conspicuous among them was a gentleman whom everybody took to be an artist because of the combination of straggling beard, green suit, brick-coloured shirt and yellow tie.

Though the Constitution Hill gate and the Grosvenor Place gate are both open, leading directly into the gardens, most people prefer to go in through the main entrance, thus catching a brief glimpse of some of the interior of the Palace as they go through. They enter by way of the Grand Hall, then pass into the Bow Room. Here it was that Queen Victoria, a hundred years ago, made known to her Privy Council her intention to marry Prince Albert. It is one of the pleasantest rooms in the Palace with a large bay, the windows of which overlook the gardens and give exit to the wide terrace.

The expansive lawn—not so green as in other years when there has been more rain but parched now and with much light brown about it—soon began to fill up as the guests streamed in.

Diplomatically, the diplomats are invited in alphabetical order. For to-day's party, the latters ranged from A to L with the Afghan and Argentine representatives heading the list. Those from "L" onwards will come to the second party later this month. Members of the Corps Diplomatique and others having what is known as "the privilege of the Entree" arrive by way of a special entrance at the side of the Palace, thus avoiding any congestion there may be at the main entrance. They also have a separate tea enclosure.

The arrangements do not vary from party to party or from year to year. The invariable proceeding is that the King and Queen come out to join their guests about four o'clock, as they did this afternoon. With them were the two Princesses, the Duke of Edinburgh, the Duke and Duchess of Gloucester and the Duchess of Kent.

The Queen was wearing one of her favourite colours, powder blue, with a broad-brimmed light straw hat. She carried a pale blue feather boa. Princess Elizabeth was in a dress of shepherds plaid tie silk with a grey silk coat which was edged with white. Princess Margaret looked charming in clover pink. The King, like the Duke of Edinburgh, was in naval uniform. Queen Mary, who has found the recent hot weather tiring, was not present.

The band played the National Anthem when the Royal party came out—and that was the only note of ceremony there was throughout the afternoon. It was also the signal to the waitresses that they might now begin serving tea.

Gentlemen ushers, red carnations in

their button holes, formed narrow lanes through the throng of guests along which passed the King and Queen, taking separate ways, with their attendants. The Lord Chamberlain preceded the King. This was, however, no formal procession but more of a friendly stroll. At every few steps someone would be presented—a visitor from overseas, perhaps—to find, as so many people on so many occasions have commented before, that the King and Queen are very kind " and make you feel so very much at home." Here and there, too, recognizing a familiar face, they would stop to renew an acquaintance. Princess Margaret demurely accompanied the Queen. Princess Elizabeth and the Duke of Edinburgh walked together among the guests, talking to many of them.

Everyone kept looking apprehensively at the sky and a tall and hovering police officer in morning clothes was to be seen dangling Princess Elizabeth's short umbrella from his wrist. But the rain held off and it was not required.

The King and Queen and the other members of the Royal Family, having spent an hour in this way among the general company, linked up again in their marquee to which privileged guests are invited.

The small tea tables set out on the lawn were now all occupied. In the long refreshment pavilion, the waitresses were busy serving guests. There were bridge rolls, gateaux, white and brown bread and butter, Swiss roll and cut cake ; tea and iced coffee, orange and lemon squash. The raspberries and cream of pre-war days have not yet made their reappearance. One helps oneself to the eatables ; the Nippies pour out the tea and the cold drinks. Catering for six thousand is a task beyond the resources of the Household staff, so a firm holding the Royal Warrant is called in. Household servants, however, are always in attendance in the Royal marquee.

Many of the guests, taking the opportunity of seeing what is behind those high spiked walls of Buckingham Palace, strolled beside the lake and wandered under the trees that give some parts of this forty-acre garden the appearance of a woodland glade. In an earlier reign, some practice golf was not entirely unknown here. In one of the far corners is a tennis court. One has no sense in this quiet garden of being in the heart of London. The noise of the traffic hardly reaches this secluded spot.

The afternoon moved leisurely on. Two bands played alternately, one that of the Irish Guards and the other the Metropolitan Police Central Band. More people were presented to the King and Queen under the ornate canopy which was once used at an Indian durbar and is brought out for every garden party. Then, shortly after six o'clock, Their Majesties returned to the Palace through another long lane of guests stretching across the lawn.

FRIDAY, JULY 8, 1949. On the barrack square of the Guards Depot at Caterham, which stands just off the main London to Brighton road a few miles beyond Croydon airport, the Colonel of the Grenadier Guards, Princess Elizabeth, to-day inspected a company of young recruits and welcomed them to the Regiment. She was dressed in the lime-green costume that she wore at Wellington Barracks a few Sundays ago.

The recruits paraded before her—volunteers and lads called up for their period of national service—in the morning sunshine. The British guardsman is not turned out in a day and none of these youths had seen much service. But they were fine material for the regiment, it was clear ; tall and straight and well-shouldered, with good clean-cut faces and steady eyes. Their rough leather army boots shone with the bright polish that only comes from hours of " elbow-grease." No professional valet could have

Photo: Daily Graphic

Princess Elizabeth and the Grenadier recruits. She is about to join them for a group photograph.

improved upon the knife-like creases of their battle dress.

"Fourteenth Company, Grenadier Guards, ready for your inspection, ma'am," said the Company commander, marching to the front of the small platform where the Princess had been received with a Royal Salute. The Colonel of the Grenadiers, followed by her Lady-in-Waiting and her Comptroller, Lieutenant-General Sir Frederick Browning, walked slowly along the ranks. She noted each man carefully and separately. Here and there she stopped to address one of them. Then she returned to the platform.

"You will find in the regiment a spirit of comradeship and a standard to live up to which will remain with you all your lives, whether your service with us be long or short," said the Princess, glancing round the squads of tall young men. "I know that the training which you will undergo is a hard one, but there are few worth-while achievements that can be reached by the easy road. It is not for nothing that the Grenadiers have won their high reputation for discipline, devotion to duty and courage in the field. I have not the slightest doubt that you will sustain that reputation . . . I wish you all success in your training and I look forward to meeting you again as fully-fledged Grenadiers. Meanwhile, I can assure you that a warm and friendly welcome awaits you in the regiment."

It is, surely, not often that recruits are received into any army as were these young men at Caterham.

The Colonel-Princess, inspecting two of the rooms in the Elizabeth barrack block, found that those at Buckingham Palace, though more decorative, could not have been more spotless. Even the swabbing buckets were polished like silver.

Above the recruits' iron bedsteads, where their kits were laid out, neat as a window display, were inscribed the regiment's

battle honours : Blenheim 1704 . . . Mal-
plaquet 1709 . . . Waterloo 1815 . . .
Khartoum 1898 . . . Loos 1915 . . .
Cambrai 1917. There were many others
down the years.

MONDAY, JULY 11, 1949. In these two
months of June and July, the engagements
yearly reach their peak ; there is little
spare time. To-day provided another
example of the infinite variety of matters

Photo : Daily Graphic

July 8 : A charming study of Princess Margaret at the reception and ball in aid of
the diamond jubilee appeal of the Queen's Institute of District Nursing. Standing
behind her is the Earl of Athlone.

and events that daily now claim the attention and support of members of the Royal Family.

At noon, the King returned with the Queen from the quiet of Windsor and, half an hour later, was holding a Privy Council at the Palace. Ministers attending the Council reported that the London docks strike, now in its fifteenth day, continued. The dockers and stevedores had voted against a return to work. Thereupon, the King signed a proclamation declaring a state of emergency. Within a few hours, his attention was being claimed by the Colonial Exhibition at Marble Arch which he had promised to attend. He had made an important speech three weeks ago in inaugurating " Colonial Month." It is evidence of the measure of recovery His Majesty has made since his operation that he is now undertaking these engagements. He stayed an hour at the Exhibition, walking round. The Queen accompanied him.

Meanwhile, adding to the day's assortment of engagements, Princess Elizabeth, who is President of the Royal Society of Arts, was opening that Society's Exhibition of Humorous Art at Adelphi ; Princess Margaret was praised for her speech in addressing two hundred students at a London County Council training college for teachers at Eltham ; and the Duke of Edinburgh was preparing to open another boys' club. The Duke of Gloucester had two widely differing public duties to perform and the Princess Royal was presiding at a meeting of the A.T.S. Benevolent Fund Committee. There was, as always, more paper work to keep the King at his desk.

There are few things in life more important than a sense of humour, said Princess Elizabeth at the art exhibition. " I might be accused of exaggeration if I said that the Englishman's—and, of course, the Scotsman's —ability to laugh at himself has won us an empire ; but I am sure it has contributed a good deal towards keeping it together, and it certainly did much to win our victories in the two world wars," she added. Pausing in front of H. M. Bateman's famous picture of the Guardsman who dropped his rifle on parade, the Princess asked the artist who was standing at her side : " Have you ever seen that happen ? " Mr. Bateman replied that he had not. " I have," said the Princess. " It's just like that ! " And, as Colonel of the Grenadiers, she confessed in her speech, " I am frequently haunted by the thought of the Guardsman who Dropped It."

It was in a side street in Fulham that the Duke of Edinburgh opened the hutted Brunswick boys' club, a place which is a monument to unselfishness. But it was in a prisoner-of-war camp in Germany—in Oflag 79, near Brunswick, housing three thousand half-starved officers and men— that the scheme for the club had its beginnings. In this squalid camp, crowded together in the bombed shells of buildings, living chiefly on turnip soup and rye bread, cold and hungry, these men decided that they would found and endow a boys' club. It was to be a challenge and a memorial ; a challenge to the wasted years of imprisonment and a memorial to their friends who had been killed in the war. One might imagine, said the Duke, that people who had spent a long time in forcible confinement would have been inclined to lose faith in the future but these men had shown that they had a very strong faith.

Most of them were British and Empire troops. There were also some Americans. All of them had been taken in battle. Many had been wounded. How many of them, one wonders, could have envisaged this Fulham scene as they made their plans in the winter cold of the prison camp ?

There were more Union Jacks along the street than it has ever seen before. The Prime Minister found time amid all the worries of the dock strike to slip in and

The King enters his car at the end of a visit with the Queen to the Colonial Exhibition in London.

Princess Elizabeth, President of the Royal Society of Arts, is amused by a drawing at the
exhibition of humorous art.

make a short speech. Everybody thought that was a very fine gesture. The club itself, built on a site where bombs had left a great gap in the trim Fulham houses, was in full working order under the charge of a cheerful-looking ex-parachutist who had been captured at the battle of Arnhem.

At this opening ceremony, many of the ex-P.O.W.s met again for the first time since they were flown home from Germany after their liberation. About a hundred of them who had been " in the bag ", as they call it, at Oflag 79 turned up. They were the cheeriest-looking lot of men you would meet in a day's march. " It's good to see you again," they said to one another as they shook hands. There was no searching for names. They all remembered one another very clearly.

The colonel who presided, as chairman of the club's trustees, had been one of them. He had recently been to Brunswick. " You may be surprised to know that the place we knew is still a prison camp," he said. " It's the ' cooler ' for the Rhine Army. As I walked across the compound, one young rascal came across with a couple of pails of whitewash. I stopped him and said : ' What's it like here ? ' ' Oh, I've been in worse,' he said. I told him : ' I spent nine months here '. With respect dawning in his eyes for the first time, he asked :

'What did they nail yer for, chum?'"

The Duke spoke, praising the example that these men had shown, and unveiled a tablet. The Prime Minister said he thought a club such as this was a very good school of citizenship and leadership—"the right kind of leadership, not the leadership that just orders people about but leadership that just influences other people and so gets them to follow."

A padre who had been " in the bag " dedicated the club. Having seen this fulfilment of their plans, the ex-prisoners of war went their separate ways again.

Photo: Associated Press

The Duke of Edinburgh throwing the javelin at the Outward Bound School's sports at Aberdovey. He hurled it 109 feet, winning a silver star award.

THIRTY FOUR WEEKS OLD

Prince Charles of Edinburgh was thirty four weeks old when these delightfully informal photographs were taken at Windlesham Moor, near Sunningdale, the country home of Princess Elizabeth and the Duke of Edinburgh.

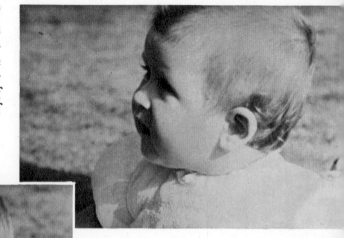

Photographs by Mr. Graham Thompson, of the Newsreel Association of Great Britain and Ireland.

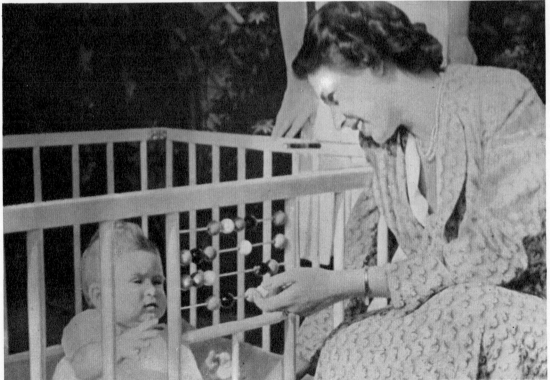

WEDNESDAY, JULY 20, 1949. Charles Lamb, son of a waiter in the Inner Temple Hall, sitting down to pen for the *London Magazine* of 1821 that delightful essay on the old Benchers who paraded so impressively before his childish eyes, wrote with affection of " cheerful Crown Office Row ". It was the place of his " kindly engendure," for he was born in the Temple and passed the first seven years of his life amidst the lawyers there, as he tells us in the essay's opening sentence. " Indeed, it is the most elegant spot in the metropolis," said the essayist. He pictured the transition for a countryman visiting London for the first time and passing by way of unexpected avenues from the crowded Strand or Fleet Street into the Temple's " magnificent ample squares, its classic green recesses." A man would give something to have been born in such places, he declared.

Alas now, for the historic Temple. The barristers and their clerks must often sigh to themselves as, crossing between their chambers and the Law Courts on the other side of the traffic-filled Strand, they look upon the ruins left by war.

When, perforce, the tortured walls had been demolished and all the rubble cleared away, there was little that was left, excepting the name, of cheerful Crown Office Row where, in the basement of No. 3, Lamb was brought, unnoticed into the world. There used to be a stone on the outside wall, marking his birthplace.

Elsewhere, terrible damage was done to even more historic buildings, some of them of great beauty, both in the Inner Temple and the Middle Temple. All but the shell of the Temple Church was destroyed. The two fine halls were bombed and burned, though that of the Middle Temple escaped with less severe wounds than the other across the Lane. Disaster fell from the skies on the Temple's elegance and one learned judge commented in bitterness that Charles Lamb might well, perhaps, have reflected that it would be better not to be born at all in a world that was cursed with a Hitler and a Tojo, a Himmler and a Laval.

As one walks nowadays through the Temple, the builder's men, it seems, have taken charge and the noise of their hammering sounds through these quiet walks. There is a great deal of scaffolding about some of the less grievously damaged buildings that are capable of repair ; it gives them the appearance of being in splints. There are great gaps among the buildings. Weeds grow amid the ruins, where people who favour some quiet not infrequently come off the crowded streets to sit in the shade, eating their lunchtime sandwiches. Cosy little fireplaces that, one may well guess, must have seen the brewing of many a lawyer's cup of tea, stand revealed and are dotted here and there, clinging to the walls of the sliced buildings. At the open windows of some of those chambers that escaped, you may see the barristers at their work and, passing, wonder what court will hear the argument which they are now so concentratedly preparing.

When one passes out of the Strand, where the evening newspaper sellers sit all day long on their upturned wooden boxes at the entrances to the Temple lanes, and one enters this peaceful quarter, the years can readily fall away in imagination. It is not difficult, even with all this damage around and about, to conjure up the picture of Lamb's old Benchers walking here : Thomas Coventry, " whose person was a quadrate, his step massy and elephantine, his face square as the lion's, his gait peremptory and pathkeeping, indivertible from his way as a moving column " ; Samuel Salt, with his pensive gentility ; Peter Pierson, " a benevolent but not a prepossessing man " ; the omniscient Jackson and the rest.

In the centuries of its history, say the lawyers, the Temple has suffered many times from fire and destruction and what has been lost has been restored and rebuilt.

That task is now being faced again in the confidence that, once more, this will become the most elegant place in the metropolis.

This has been a Royal year for the two Honourable Societies of the Inner Temple and the Middle Temple, for the King is Treasurer, for the period, of the first-named and the Queen holds similar office in the other. Their Majesties have each been separately to the Temple this month and, on the occasion of the joint Bench dinner to-night, were present together.

At the beginning of the month, the Queen reopened the restored Middle Temple Hall. On that afternoon, it might have been noticed, certain High Court Judges who were attending this happy ceremony and the subsequent garden party, adjourned their courts a little before the customary hour and joined their fellow lawyers of the Inn. The Queen's speech charmed them all, who must have listened to, and made, so many speeches. I give it here in full, so excellent is its pattern and so sincere its sentiment :

" I am very grateful to you, Master Deputy Treasurer, for the kind words you have used. It is a great pleasure to me to be here to-day and, as Treasurer, to welcome the many guests whom I see in our Hall.

" Whilst our Benchers are drawn, of course, from those who have made the Law their study, it has always been our practice to add distinction to our ranks by including within them leaders of the Church and State, the fighting services and the world of Letters.

" I am happy to see that a tradition which found Drake and Hawkins among its earliest examples, and General Smuts among its more recent, is still continued today, and that we have among our friends this afternoon many who can claim distinctions of infinite variety outside the practice of the Law.

" What unites them, I am sure, is their desire to pay their tribute to the Honourable Society of the Middle Temple, and to join with its members on this occasion of thanksgiving and rejoicing.

" That, I think, is a very proper purpose, for in all the complex fabric of our national life, nothing transcends in its importance the dignity and authority of the Law. It touches every one of us, and it was the intention to repudiate the Rule of Law, and to replace it by a monstrous tyranny, which brought to us these wounds which, as we may see all about us, were so nearly mortal.

" As we count our scars and those of our near neighbours and good friends across Middle Temple Lane, we may well marvel that this lovely hall, begun nearly four hundred years ago, still stands proud and undismayed, like a jewel in a broken setting.

" So brilliantly has its restoration been effected that it is easy to forget the problems which faced those who were charged with this work. Let me recall them to you.

" In October, 1940, the explosion of a landmine hurled a huge piece of masonry through the east end behind you, smashing the Gallery and burying our famed oak screen beneath a mass of rubble. Part of the Clock Tower was demolished and the East Wall was shattered, with two adjacent windows and much of the panelling. Happily, most of the hammer beam roof remained intact, but in March of 1944 this, too, was set ablaze by incendiaries. The cupola was burned out but, largely owing to the devoted labours of our fire-watchers, the flames were controlled and the roof saved.

" Broken fragments have now been lovingly reassembled ; in the roof new oak has been inserted, and to-day our hall shows, as we may see, a new strength and a new beauty. Its successful accomplishment may seem to those who have carried out this great work to be their most fitting and sufficient reward but I should like, on behalf of us all, to express our admiration and our gratitude to our architect and to the faithful craftsmen under his direction.

" The great table, made from oak sent from Windsor by the direction of Queen Elizabeth, stands again behind me. This other table, called ' The Cupboard ', was made from a hatch of the ' Golden Hind', and given to his brethren of this Inn by Sir Francis Drake on his return from circumnavigating the world. It, too, has returned, unscathed and welcome. We may well be thankful for so much good fortune.

" With our thankfulness and rejoicing, may we not also draw inspiration from our experience, and believe that if we face danger and peril, however merciless, with an unwavering courage and a sure faith, justice and freedom will still be our reward ; and, after much suffering —peace.

" In that hope, and in humble confidence, it is now my great happiness to declare our lovely hall open once again."

Then, a week later, the other royal Treasurer, the King, attended to open rooms of the Inner Temple temporary library, an occasion on which there was some slight financial juggling with a penny given in exchange for the pair of scissors with which His Majesty was presented to cut the ribbon stretched across the doorway. As far as one could gather, the lawyers had a penny ready along with the scissors. The King, however, decided that that would not be in order if the tradition were to be properly observed. So, having no pennies himself, he borrowed a coin from his Private Secretary and this he duly handed over. After the informal opening ceremony, the King remained for a considerable time to meet members of the Inn.

At the joint dinner, held to-night with pleasant ceremony in the reopened Middle Temple Hall, the Queen proposed the King's health and then His Majesty rose to give the health of the Queen. Each spoke again, doing honour to the other's Inn, on this unique occasion. Together, they inspected the Charter granted by James the First in 1608 under which the two Inns hold most of their property, and signed a document stating that they had found the Charter intact.

Photo: P.A.-Reuter

July 20 : Princess Margaret at the London wedding of Lady Elizabeth Lambart, daughter of the late Earl of Cavan.

July 20 : Princess Elizabeth arriving at St. Peter's Church, Eaton Square, London, for the wedding of Lady Elizabeth Lambart. The bride was one of her bridesmaids.

Photo: A. T. Gill

July 20 : The Duke and Duchess of Gloucester at the Summer Show of the Peterborough Agricultural Society. The Duke takes a keen interest nowadays in farming.

Photo: Keystone

July 21 : A Palace garden party. The King and Queen with Queen Mary, the two Princesses, the Duke of Edinburgh and other members of the Royal Family returning through a " lane " of guests to the Palace.

FRIDAY, JULY 22, 1949. The two hundred and thirty schoolteachers who gathered this afternoon on the lawn of Lambeth Palace came from many parts of the world. Some of them had their homes in the cities of Australia, others had travelled across the prairies of Canada to take ship for England. There were New Zealanders and South Africans. Over a hundred of them came from the United States of America ; from New York and the Middle West and the South. Nearly all of them were women. Some were young but, mostly, they were middle-aged. They all fell beneath the spell of the Queen's charm. They had never, they said, met anyone more gracious. They were glad she had come in blue because that was how they always thought of her, dressed in blue.

They were, most of them, a little nervous about the prospect of having to curtsey before the Queen and more than a few preliminary practisings were to be seen going on in corners of the Archbishop's lawn. Said one American teacher who was anxious to know whether the right foot was placed behind the left—or was it the left behind the right ?—" We don't go in for this much back home in the States." For a moment she was as apprehensive as one of her backward pupils, about to be confronted with the term's examination papers. She was praying, she said, that she would not fall over.

This atmosphere was dispelled within a minute when the Queen came out on to the lawn. She wore a summer dress of delphinium blue. The Archbishop of

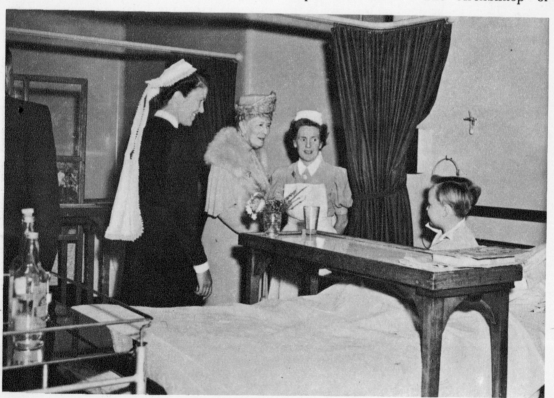

Photo: London News Agency

July 19 : Queen Mary has a talk with a young patient at London Hospital, of which she is Patron.

Canterbury, Dr. Fisher, accompanied her. The Queen looked round at the school-teachers, waiting for her on the lawn. Then she smiled. Painters cannot capture the qualities of the Queen's smile. Nor do the photographs ever fully express it. It is a young, gay smile. It shines in the eyes like summer sunshine dancing on blue water. It has a friendliness about it that clearly says: "*Please don't be anxious or worried because I am the Queen.*" There are no shades to its warmth. It rests with equal kindliness upon everyone, high and low alike. It was a young American woman, a teacher in high school at Chappagna, Westchester County, who said at this moment, "I think it is the most lovely smile I have ever seen."

One by one, the teachers passed in front of the Queen as she stood on the lawn in the shade of a tree. She spoke to them about their work and their home countries, asked questions about the schools in which, under exchange schemes, they had been teaching over here. She talked longest of all with the single coloured woman present, a teacher from a kindergarten in Indiana who had been taking classes in the Paddington area of London.

The teachers replied in accents that were almost as varied as the colours and styles of their garden party dresses. At the Queen's side, the Archbishop beamed benignly. No one was the least bit nervous now. And all the curtsies were safely achieved. Then there was tea in the marquees.

Some of the teachers had the opportunity of another talk with the Queen as she walked across the lawn afterwards. They

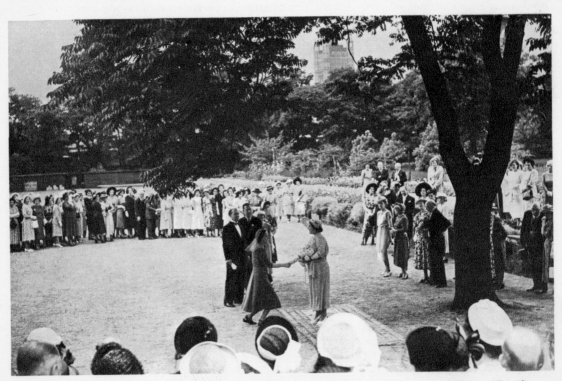

Photo: The Times

The overseas teachers pass before the Queen, making their curtseys, on the Archbishop's lawn at Lambeth Palace.

were all deeply sensible of the fact that, on such a hot and tiring day, she had spent so much time with them. To Miss Dorothy Lea, an Australian from Sydney, the Queen talked about her grandson, Prince Charles. The people of Australia, said Miss Lea, were very interested in the infant Prince.

"Babies bring the world together," said the Queen.

TUESDAY, JULY 26, 1949. Albert Cook spends most of his days checking electrical accessories in a Shoreditch factory and most of his leisure hours in the small back garden of his house in Warner Place, Bethnal Green. He grows many varieties of flowers. "But tomatoes are my speciality," he says. Last year, he gathered 362 lbs.

Gardening for Mr. Cook, a man in middle age, is not only a hobby; it is a passion. Long ago, before he moved into No. 88, set in the low row of uniform houses that is Warner Place, E.2., he and his wife lived in two rented rooms nearby. Looking out from their windows, they used to sigh : "If only we could have a garden." Then No. 88 became vacant. Mr. and Mrs. Cook moved in. Soon the garden began to bloom with Albert Cook's flowers. They have been blooming there ever since.

A week or so ago, Mrs. Buckland, who is the Honorary Secretary of the Bethnal Green Gardens Guild, calling at No. 88, asked Mrs. Cook if she might bring a few friends round to look at the garden ; it was a picture, she said.

"Bring them any day you like except on Monday, because that's my washing day," said Mrs. Cook.

This evening, five minutes before the royal car drove up to the door of No. 88, the Secretary told Mrs. Cook, whose husband had just got home from work : "*Your visitor is the Queen.*"

"I felt a little bit nervous at first but, after that, I sort of braved to it," said the housewife afterwards. All her trepidation vanished, though, when the great moment came. For, when the Queen stood at the front door of No. 88, asking "May I come in ? ", Mrs. Cook said she felt it was like having one of her friends come to see her.

The housewife took the Queen through the kitchen and the neat scullery out into the garden. "How lovely !" exclaimed the Queen when she saw the result of Albert Cook's long hours of work. Neighbours living in "pre-fabs," peered over the garden fence. The Queen had a friendly word with them, too, as she went round admiring the gladioli, the antirrhinums, the ten-weeks stocks and all the rest of the flowers. The man living in the house next door confessed to her over the fence that he was no gardener. "That's the wife's hobby," he said. "Mine's rabbits."

The Cooks' garden is about the length of a cricket pitch and only six yards wide. Every inch of space was filled. Even the Anderson bomb shelter was covered with multi-coloured blooms. It looked very different now from the night when a bomb fell nearby and the Cooks were trapped inside for half an hour before rescuers got them out ("I shall never forget someone's piano landing right on top of it, with all the notes going," recalls the amateur gardener of Warner Place).

There were two peach trees grown from stones and a great show of outdoor tomatoes. Each separate truss of green fruit was neatly held up by white tape. Roses enclosed the garden on all sides.

"I shall often think of you in your lovely garden," said the Queen to Mr. and Mrs. Cook when she left them to continue her evening tour of these unexpected gardens in the City and the East End.

Mr. Brandi, the shoemaker, he, too, showed the Queen his flowers. They bloom in the cellars, now open to the sky, of some bombed premises not far from St. Paul's

The Queen chatting with Mrs. Cook in the garden at Warner Place, Bethnal Green,
during her tour of some of London's back gardens.

Cathedral. Ingenious Mr. Brandi brought up mud from the Thames and mixed it with sand from his war-time sandbags.

Near the gasometers, at the tenement dwellings of the Stepney Housing Trust, there were many window boxes to be admired.

Then there was the old people's flower show at Hoxton Hall. Here in this poor neighbourhood, they sang for the Queen :

There's a bit of Old London we think is grand
It's not Piccadilly or down the Strand.
Tucked away and it's hard to find

But the folks who live there are good and kind.
They don't wear fine clothes or drive motor-cars
And they live by the sweat of their brow.
But come up and see us any old time,
You'll get such a Welcome, I vow.

Earlier in the day, at Buckingham Palace, the King, amid many duties, had held a short investiture. It lasted only three-quarters of an hour and he stood throughout the ceremony. People in many walks of life were among the 138 men and women whom His Majesty invested and decorated.

Photo: Keystone

After the investiture on July 26. Constable George Lloyd and Sgt. J. F. Barclay of Glasgow leaving the palace after receiving the King's Police and Fire Service Medals for Gallantry.

WEDNESDAY, JULY 27, 1949. The King presented new Colours to the 1st Battalion of the Irish Guards in the garden of the Palace this morning. Field Marshal Viscount Alexander, who is Colonel of the Regiment, flew from Canada for the ceremony.

His Majesty paid tribute to the exploits and sacrifices, not only of the 1st Battalion, but of the whole Regiment during the war years. " I am glad to see plainly to-day that the scars of battle, of which you have borne your full share, have left no mark upon your spirit," he said. " In a world of change, your courage and discipline remain unchanged."

To-night, attending a reception given by the Pakistan High Commissioner and his wife at new premises in Lowndes Square, the King and Queen were presented with garlands of gold thread flown from Pakistan.

FRIDAY, JULY 29, 1949. Princess Elizabeth and the Duke of Edinburgh ended another of their joint tours yesterday. This time they visited Yorkshire but, as the Duke said in a speech at Harrogate, trying to see the West Riding in three days reminded him of the American tourist who said he was going to see Rome in the afternoon.

A colleague who accompanied the official party returned to tell of vast crowds and

Photo: *Photographic News*

The Queen is presented with a garland of gold thread at the Pakistan High Commissioner's reception.

The King photographed with Field Marshal Viscount Alexander of Tunis on the garden terrace of Buckingham Palace. The King had presented new colours to the 1st Battalion of the Irish Guards. Viscount Alexander is Colonel of the Regiment.

tremendous receptions everywhere. It was his first experience of a Royal tour and he found it arduous.

A beflagged and excited Halifax was the first Yorkshire town to greet the visitors. The crowds outside the Huddersfield Town Hall, who had been singing "On Ilkla Moor Bah't 'At," were amused to note that the Duke was carrying his bowler when he arrived. He invariably does. Indeed, I cannot recall ever having seen him put it on. The day ended at Pudsey where the Mayor described the Princess and the Duke as "the most popular married couple in the British Empire at the present time."

This was an eight-and-a-half hours day. Wednesday's programme was even longer.

Leeds, in the morning, and Wakefield, in the afternoon, each staged a wonderful welcome. At night, at the Harrogate dinner, the Chairman of the West Riding County Council tendered "a warm Yorkshire welcome of loyalty, respect and affection."

Historic York was visited yesterday and, amid the visit to the Minster and all else that happened during the day in this ancient city, the incident that caught the imagination most occurred during a tour of inspection of some working-class Council homes. Here, in a prefabricated house, the Princess and the Duke were to be found most happily sitting down to tea with a bus driver and his family.

Photo: P.A.-Reuter

August 4 : Relaxation at the end of a busy round of public engagements. Princess Elizabeth in "slacks", with the Duke of Edinburgh watching the racing at Cowes. The yacht, *Fanny Rosa*, belongs to Lt.-General Sir Frederick Browning, the Princess's Comptroller.

Princess Elizabeth attends
a dinner at Harrogate
during the Yorkshire tour.

Photo: Yorkshire Post

AUGUST IN THE HIGHLANDS

THURSDAY, AUGUST 4, 1949. To-day, the Queen, celebrating her 49th birthday, received many greetings at the Palace. To-night, there was a family outing to the theatre to see the amusing Sid Field in " Harvey," the play about a man with an imaginary rabbit. Princess Elizabeth and Princess Margaret accompanied their parents with the Duke of Edinburgh. There was a great stir of excitement throughout the theatre when the Queen led the party to their seats in the front row of the stalls. The entire house rose, clapping, to its feet. When Sid Field was received and made his bow in an ante-room during one of the intervals, the King wanted to know : " Where's Harvey ? " " I didn't think I ought to bring him here, Sir," replied Field conspiratorially. So the imaginary rabbit was not presented.

The Duke of Edinburgh, it was announced to-day, is returning to sea in October. He is going as first lieutenant ("Jimmy the One " is the sailors' title) of the 1,710-tons destroyer, *Chequers*. The ship is the leader of the Mediterranean Fleet's First Destroyer Flotilla, stationed at Malta.

The Duke, as second in command, will be responsible, among other things, for the discipline and daily routine of the ship. From all that one hears from naval men with whom he has served, he is an outstanding officer who has done extremely well throughout his service with the Royal Navy.

Having been on half-pay for about a year, the Duke now goes back to sea, with the King's consent, at his own request. He is returning to duties and to a type of ship he knows well. He was only twenty-one when he rose to become first lieutenant of the destroyer, *Wallace*, during the war. She took part in the Sicily operations, covering the landings at the Canadian beach. Later, he served as " Number One " aboard the *Whelp*, then one of our latest destroyers, and saw service against the Japanese.

Having seen a good deal of the Duke as he has gone about his public duties in this country over the past year, one knows how energetically and efficiently, with what unfailing good humour and naval cheeriness he has performed each one of them. He will be greatly missed upon the royal scene while he is away at sea.

FRIDAY, AUGUST 5, 1949. At seven o'clock this evening, the King and Queen with Princess Elizabeth and Princess Margaret left London for Balmoral to spend their annual holiday in the Scottish Highlands. They travelled through the night in the royal train.

Prince Charles, now nearly nine months old and making his first train journey, was driven to Euston station in the care of his nurse, Miss Helen Lightbody, half an hour beforehand. The crowd that gathered at

Photo: *Graphic Photo Union*

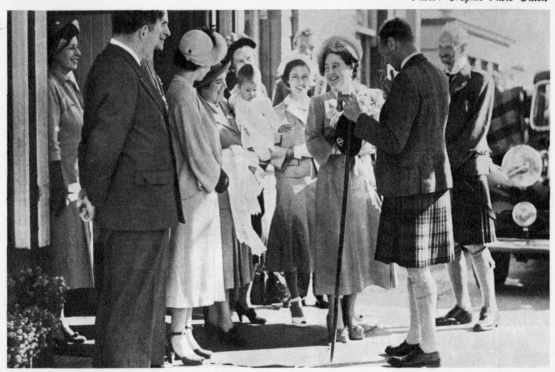

Photo: *Aberdeen Journals Ltd.*

Prince Charles, carried by his nurse, is the centre of interest when the King and Queen with the two Princesses detrain at Ballater Station to start their holiday in the Scottish Highlands.   The King wears the kilt.

the station to see the royal party leave was thrilled to catch this glimpse of him. Miss Lightbody carried the Prince from the car along the platform to the train compartment which she shared with him during the long journey north. I dare say he was fast asleep as the train pulled smoothly out, on the stroke of time.

It has been an eventful year since, last summer, one watched a similar family departure scene, though there was no Prince Charles then for the crowd to cheer. His Majesty looks very fit now and far less strained than a twelvemonth ago when he was obviously tired under the pressure of an unrelenting round of duty that had continued, without ease, for so long. Princess Elizabeth, it is not difficult to imagine, will be glad of some rest after a most strenuous summer during which she has had little time to call her own.

A thousand good wishes follow the royal party north to Scotland, where later the Duke of Edinburgh, who still has two engagements to carry out, will join his wife and son.

SUNDAY, AUGUST 14, 1949. The Minister of Crathie came walking thoughtfully across the meadows from the Manse, thinking, no doubt, of his sermon.

His small church, perched on the hillside above the winding riverside road that links Ballater and Braemar, is just across the river from Balmoral Castle. It was here, at Crathie, that Queen Victoria used to worship when she travelled north to Balmoral, her " dear Paradise," shared at first in great happiness with Prince Albert, her husband. After his death she returned there year after year, in early summer and again in the autumn. On Sundays she went to the parish church on the hillside.

As the Minister walked on, the morning sunshine sparkled on the swift-running waters of the shallow Dee, bubbling along over its pebbled bed past Balmoral. The sunshine brightened the slopes and heights of the surrounding hills that had looked so dark at breakfast-time. They are constantly changing in aspect, these rugged hills. They overawe the quiet valleys. But this morning even Lochnagar, highest of them all, which can be so darkly forbidding, was friendly and welcoming and free from mist. The heather spread its purple glow across the grandeur of the Highland scene. The pine forests were very still, for there was but little wind. It was a perfect day.

The Reverend John Lamb, Minister of Crathie and Domestic Chaplain to the King in Scotland—a silver-haired man in middle age—was dressed this morning in formal morning coat and glossy silk top hat. He climbed the rough, dusty path leading to the grey granite church and, going inside, set out the books in the royal pew.

The place is full of memories of Victoria. It was she who laid the foundation stone of the present church, built on the site of an earlier one, towards the end of the last century. She was there, sitting in the royal pew, when the building was dedicated and opened on a June day in 1895. The beautifully-designed chaste silver Communion plate bears the inscription " Presented by Her Majesty Queen Victoria to the Church of Crathie, 1871." For many years, the Queen was a regular communicant. She gave the church stained glass windows in memory of those dear to her.

Not only Balmoral, which she loved, and Crathie, but the district generally is rich in its Victorian connections. At Ballater, seven and a half miles away, where the single-line railway from Aberdeen comes to its abrupt end, there is a Victoria Hall, a Victoria Road (leading to the golf links by the river) ; even a Victoria garage. The post office in the square is housed in the Albert memorial hall building opposite the small but busy railway station. There is an Albert Road, too.

The Minister of Crathie, having seen that everything was arranged as it should be, retired to the vestry. The church, for the moment, was empty. Two vases of flowers stood behind the white and green Iona marble communion table which, with the screen made from three-hundred-years-old oak, commemorates King Edward VII. It was King Edward who placed the white marble bust of his mother in a niche in the pillar at the side of the Royal pew. The inscription reads:

In dutiful and beloved remembrance of
Victoria,
Queen of Great Britain and Ireland,
Empress of India,
This Monument is erected by her
sorrowing and devoted son,
Edward R. and I.

There is a bust, too, of King George V, placed in the church by his son, King George VI.

The bells began to toll their four tones. It was a gentle unpretentious peal as befits a hamlet church that holds no more than three hundred and fifty people. The sound of it would not carry much beyond the castle across the river. From that direction, where the soldiers were parading, came the music of the bagpipes.

Along at the post office, which is built on to a cottage on the hillside, only a few yards from the church, Albert Thomson, the postmaster, and one of the Elders of the Kirk, prepared for the morning service. His grandfather opened the post office at Crathie in 1844. The appointment has been held in the family ever since. Business used to be transacted through a front window of

Photo: Aberdeen Journals Ltd.

The King, now happily restored to health, inspects the guard of honour drawn up in the square at Ballater.

the cottage. Queen Victoria told the present postmaster's father " You must build a post office "—and so the addition to the cottage came about.

Soon, the other four Elders, the postmaster's seniors in this responsibility, arrived by their separate ways and went into the church. There was James Abercrombie, one time head stalker on the Balmoral estate, now in his eighties ; William Brown, formerly a schoolmaster at Crathie ; Sidney Dear, the present dominie ; and Ian Cowan, who is a farmer at nearby Abergeldie.

The villagers of Crathie, dressed in their Sunday best and carrying their bibles, came slowly up the hillside paths. They were admitted with a nod and a smile of recognition by the beadle or by Charles Lamont who was beadle for five and twenty years and now comes to give a helping hand on these " Royal " Sundays, wearing, as he always used to, his Highland dress and his medals. None of the visitors who had arrived by the cars and the coaches that were now parked in one of the meadows at river level was allowed in yet. The Crathie people, as everybody recognises, must all be seated first.

The church was already more than half full when the kilted young soldiers of the Highland Light Infantry marched up the slope from the Ballater-Braemar road. Each lad swept off his Balmoral bonnet as he came to the wooden church porch. The soldiers occupied seven of the remaining pews, three rows on the left of the aisle and four on the right. Then a few of the visitors were shepherded quietly in. The church door was shut.

Out from the grounds of Balmoral Castle, over the iron bridge spanning the clear waters of the Dee at a point almost opposite the church and the post office, drove the King and Queen with the two Princesses to join the Crathie folk at their morning service, as Queen Victoria used to do, commenting in her Journal when she returned on the merits of the sermons she heard.

The Minister of Crathie conducted the service without assistance, just as he does on any other Sunday. This was a parish church service, not a royal occasion. He announced the hymns and psalms, read the lessons, said the prayers. He gave the date of the sale of work that the Women's Guild are holding.

One of the hymns, " O Son of Man, our Hero strong and tender " was sung to the tune of the Londonderry Air. The young soldiers, joining in the singing, shared the hymnals provided in each pew, bunching together in threes.

From a pulpit made of eighteen different varieties of Scottish granite and set with pebbles gathered on the shores of the island of Iona, the Minister preached a sermon based on the text " *Elisha left the oxen and ran after Elijah.*" The point he made was : " It is no bad thing to go the high way instead of the low." It was a good sermon.

When the collection was taken up, the old head stalker, Abercrombie—a tall, spare man dressed in darkish green—went along the royal pew with the bag.

The service lasted about an hour. There were the customary prayers for the members of the Royal Family. Here, in this place, they had a special significance.

When it was over, the King and Queen and the Princesses drove quietly away, past all the people gathered outside ; back to the castle that Prince Albert planned for Queen Victoria. The soldiers marched away and the villagers of Crathie went home to their mid-day meal.

Inside the church, the Minister of Crathie collected the books from the royal pew, putting them away until the next Sunday, then walked back across the meadows to the manse.